Birth *of a* Notion

Birth *of a* Notion;

OR,

THE HALF AIN'T NEVER BEEN TOLD

A Narrative Account with Entertaining Passages

of the State of Minstrelsy

& of America & the True Relation Thereof

(from the Ha Ha Dark Side)

as Written by

Bill Harris

Wayne State University Press   Detroit

Library of Congress Cataloging-in-Publication Data

Harris, Bill, 1941–

Birth of a notion, or, the half ain't never been told : a narrative account with entertaining
passages of the state of Minstrelsy & of America & the true relation thereof (from the ha ha
dark side) / as written by Bill Harris.

  p. cm. — (Made in Michigan writers series)

ISBN 978-0-8143-3408-9 (pbk. : alk. paper)

1. United States—Race relations—History—Poetry. 2. African Americans—Poetry. 3.
Minstrel music. I. Title. II. Title: Birth of a notion. III. Title: Half ain't never been told.

PS3558.A6415B57 2010

811'.54—dc22

2009033732

Designed and typeset by d2do, llc, Elizabeth Youngblood

Composed in Cochin and Mesquite Std

History, real solemn history, I cannot be interested in. . . .
I read it a little as a duty; but it tells me nothing that does not either
vex or weary me. The quarrels of popes and kings, with wars and
pestilences in every page; the men all so good for nothing,
and hardly any women at all.

Jane Austen, *Northanger Abbey*

CONTENTS

PREFACE

Minstrelsy was the first pop culture entertainment phenomenon in young nineteenth-century America. It was mostly immigrant males hoping that, by performing amusing but racist portrayals of African Americans, they would throw off the stereotypical notions regarding their kind and be accepted by and as white Americans. These stereotyped impersonations have served as the template for American amusement for the masses until today. *Birth of a Notion* considers the situation from the dark side, intending to reflect the process back on itself.

The initial trickle that set the flow of *Birth of a Notion* in motion is lost in the mist of memory. Among the several possibilities for its inception are, first, my ongoing attempt to understand the influence of African American culture on American culture. Second, I was drawn to the idea of examining the enduring images of African Americans throughout American history and to understand the origins of those images, who perpetrated them, why they were necessary, and why and how they endured. And third, as a creative writer, I was experimenting in a quest to find a form and language to present an alternative scan of American history and the imagery it produced for the paying public.

Whatever the idea's origins, it had to be an other way of seeing and an other new way of saying. It was important that the form fit the content. Its structure had to be true to the improvisational nature of the tradition that it grew out of. It had to follow the logic that was shaped by its intention. It had to allow for digression or riffing on a subject or idea. It had to surprise. It had to have an emotional core that produced an emotional response. It had to be of use to the maligned for which it was intended. This meant also that it had to recognize that all history that routinely cast them as villains, victims, or nonentities was fictional in that it was based on a preconceived, subjective theme or point of view.

Historically, after the smoke of battle has cleared and the flag flutters over occupied territory, the report transmitted back to the home folk, whose taxes paid for the artillery and whose progeny served as soldiers, must be a subjective tale told to justify their sacrifice. The prime determinant in the shaping of the "history" of that exercise is the creation of a point of view that validates or at least rationalizes the carnage and expense. The basic premise decides the characters to be emphasized, the explanation of their motivation, and the chronicle of their courses of action, the resultant conflicts, and the outcome. This process of recording history—that is, tales or incidents or new remembrances—professedly true, organized around or related to a point of view, is exactly the same as the creation of a fictional narrative.

For this project, my process of research, which took place over several summers, can best be described as improvisation. Everything I encountered was read and interpreted through an ironic, wily eye. The guiding principle was a questioning of the assumption of the basic premise of the makers and recorders of much of American "history"—that is, the premise that saw everything from the exclusionary position of their so-called authority, backed up by their being, by their self-definition, the planet's most militarily, sociologically, morally, and technologically advanced civilization.

The final form that emerged over many, many drafts is one in keeping with the jazz and blues esthetic. These classic African American music forms are nothing if not optimistic even in the (false) face of their toughest opposition. The blues, in plainspoken images and with metaphoric clarity, verbalizes its endurance against its worst fears while looking the devil in the eye and pulling its tail at the same time. In *Birth of a Notion* I hope I have retained the energy, sarcastic humor, and celebratory core of the forms the blues and jazz have appropriated. (Nudge nudge.)

INTRODUCTION

In the Beginning

From
New World's
NO nEGROES!
to
the New Negro:
a pome
in the form
of a Battle Royale,
featuring
Scott Joplin, Frederick Douglass, William Tecumseh Sherman,
Comte de Garcon, Grover Cleveland, Little Egypt, Eadweard
   Muybridge,
Minstrelsy, Andrew Jackson, Thomas Jefferson, Cinque,
P. T. Barnum, Buffalo Bill, Ragtime, the White City, the Blues
& a Host of
other
initiators
& imitators

all doing their numbers
in syncopated time,
as music, dance & film
square off
in a pop culture showdown
for all the cat's-eyes, aggies,
& peewees in the pot.

(The following epigrams are to be run on a continuous loop)

"Deceive and eat." William Carlos Williams. *"The business*

of America *is business."* Calvin Coolidge. *"There's no business
like show business."* Irving Berlin. *"History is a nightmare from which I'm
trying to awake."* Stephen Dedalus. *"How could a mess such as this
happen in America?"* Anonymous. & *"How come it's so dark?"* The spirit,
if not the words of Mantan Moreland. *"The past is never dead. It's not
even past."* William Faulkner. *"Deceive and eat."* (&c., &c. & ON & ON
. . .)

—DISCLAIMER: This is the only sentence in this pome in which
the words post-modern, post-structuralist, hegemony, discourse,
praxis, pedagogy, seminal, or trope will appear. Neither will there be
mention of binary, nor codify nor demythologize.

(If, in the above you detect or even suspect sarcasm,
or signifying, please proceed with what I'm leading you to.)

CHAPTER

Treats of the Parallel Rise

of the Industrial Revolution,

the Blues, Radical Abolitionism &

Mechanical & Martial Time

Now
on with the show;

let the pome begin:
                        See,
Gentle Reader,

the Light
slowly dawn
on
the 1890s. See
how
now A-
MERICA is in the in-
fancy of its In-
dustrialization.

Hear
the up
beat
down

beat, the
heartening signature sound, the cultural keystone, the standard of
entertainment (since the 1830s),
in every village & hamlet, every
borough, burg &
town worth its
Stars and Stripes,
the music most popular,
the hardy pace-setting, infectious, militaristic, patriotic, morale-lifting,
processional sound. See
the citizenry,
parading like Hamelin's enchanted heirs,
in the snares of its brass band mania,
marching in the communal quickstep, *ONE*, 2,
THREE, 4, DAAA
da dada *da* dada *da*
umpp! umpp!
dada *da* dada *da* dada *daaa da*
umpp! umpp! *umpp*! umpp!
of a Sousa march, *ONE*, 2
THREE, 4: All
A-
MERICAN John Philip:
1854–1932
of (Note
the irony . . .) Portuguese & German parents. See

the North. See
the mechanizing cities on the hill. See
the smoking furnaces of gritty, glowing
factories fueling by the recent war's
demands.

Fired by coal.

For now, just look away, look away, look
away to Dixie's lands.

Hear,
from as far back as the 1600s
(when o'er in Merry Ole,
Black Masques &
Othello were vogue-pop)
& the (little noted, much misread) field hollers,
& protest & work & play & social
& sacred songs
were congealing into the
primal ooze of the blues.

The blues.
"A feeling."
   For the blues was without form,
& negroid; & deep was the darkness
upon its face, & heavy the weight
upon its soul. But its Spirit was
a harkening back & a hankering forth,
& it was intimate; & it *was*
individually universal &
insistent as heartbeats, or the
Mississippi's course & surge, Two, 3, *Four.*

Why? the question is, was it? What workings,
what source? what urgency, paucity, dearth,
privation, what unfulfilled need sires
this dark art?
    & then there's the question of
the timing simultaneity. Is't
serendipity? Perchance
happenstance? Happenstance
perchance? This phenomenal, seemingly
synchronous geneses of the blues
& Industrialization.
The blues.
   "The music," scholar W. E. B.
Du Bois (1868–1963) says,

*"of an unhappy people, of the children of
disappointment; they tell of death and suffering
and unvoiced longing toward a truer world,
of misty wanderings and hidden ways."*

The blues.

"Not music,"
Southern sages assert, *"so much as in-
describably uncultivated off-
beat, nigger-lazy slurrings; downbeat &
crude groaning-moaning calls to console a
No-body cares 'bout de troubles I'se seed
soul."*

See the South (once again) turn
a deaf ear & blind eye to a future force,
as it had some 6 decades before, while
still A-MERICA's Cradle of Power,
beholding, then with arrogant apathy,
the dawn of Industrialization:

the time in A-MERICA of change
that changes A-MERICA
& Time,

Tick Tock.
Machine for man, Tick Tock Tick Tock.
Factory for cottage, Tick Tock Tick Tock.
Urban for rural, Tick Tock Tick Tock.
Capitalist for landowner, Tick Tock.

Massed goods-makers make the
move to the new Movement,
& their retooled worker-consumers
March to the tune TOOT! TOOT!
& Ding Dong & Tick Tock of factory whistles,
mill's bells & clocks.

{ Bill Harris }

Clocks
(mechanical gear for measuring or denoting time, whose operation
depends on a constant mechanical oscillator by means of which the
energy stored advances an indicator at a controlled rate. Tick Tock
Tick Tock).
Clocks.
Manufactured-in-the-North
clocks,
one of A-MERICA's first mass-produced goods.
See the pendulum swing Tick Tock.
From nature's natural to Industry's dictums,
&,
as if its time isn't running out, see
the South,
soothed by the sounds of the same old oscillating
groan, grunt & sigh of an economy based on
unrecompensed bondage.
                        See the South disregard,
though much malign, the hiss, whir, chug & grind of the
North's mechanization.
                        See the South try to hold
back the hands of time, Tick Tock Tick Tock . . . & the North
try to assuage the hourly wage.

                                    On time,
social philosopher, political
theorist, German, Karl Marx (1818–

1883) will, in 1847
say, *"We should not say that one man's hour is worth
another man's hour, but rather that one man
during an hour is worth just as much as
another man during an hour. Time,"* he will
conclude, *"is everything, man is nothing:
he is at the most time's carcass."*
Tick Tock.
See the shadowing shroud of cheap Northern
mill-made cloth.
See the price on the South's cotton crop
                                        drop
like a rock-a-bye baby from the treetop
(18 cents a yard
in 1820 to 2 cents per 4
decades later) . . .
Hear,

the matching measure of the South whistling Dixie
to the optimistic *ONE 2 THREE 4* of an
up-beat-close-order-drill Sousa march heralding
the present as their plumped pillow, & so it would
ever be.

& the concurrent apprehensive
1 Two 3 Four of a down-beat-low-country-
down-home-blues proclaiming things will not be, no they
won't; won't be this way always. See? See the insular,
autocratic, bright blue antebellum sky darkened
by the coinciding rise of the tarrying cloud
of Radical Abolitionism.

CHAPTER

2

 Treats on the Parallel Rise of

Radical Abolitionism,

American-Born Blackface,

Immigrant Upper-Lower & Lower-Middle Classes,

and Their Indoctrination in the Ways of American Life

& Free-time & How to Spend It

1831

———◦•◦———

In 1831, February (later, nudge nudge, Negro History Month), the
moon
blackens
the face of the sun.

In August of that year, Nat Turner (b.
1800) — who has, but is 3 decades too
early to have his wounds of slavery balmed
by the oil of the yet unreaped & unpressed seed
of the blues & believing the eclipse a sign —
hears God's call. Heeds, as he hears & heeds the drums in/
of his heart. TA DOOM BOOM BI-A BOOM BI-A
TA DOOM BI-A BI-A BOOM. TA DOOM BOOM BI-A BI-A
BOOM.
Upwards of 150 die; & there
is in 1831 a tremble
& a trepidation that runs under the whole

of the Southern heaven & through the dear ol' South-
land's heart, as if the Grim Reaper, awakened from
the stillness of Time, has stepped over its grave. &
the specters are called Abolitionists. & they
are mostly free blacks. & they beget a Movement,
whose truth, UMPH UMPH, begins marching on ONE, 2, THREE,
4.

> END ALL SLAVERY
> NOW!
> formerly indentured, immediast

> William Lloyd Garrison
> (1805–1879)
> demands in
> THE LIBERATOR,
> his antislavery newspaper
> (founded in 1831)

1831, the year of telegraphy, chloroform & the electric dynamo;
1831 & the mechanical reaper of Cyrus Hall McCormick (1809–
1884), getting the manpower of 5 from 1. Doodah. The year of the
determination of magnetic north.
(In their determination runaways from the reaper of slavery use the
North Star as their magnet.)

& 1831, the year liberal unrest & revolution continue on the wings of
a restless current scattering its hopeful seeds to the winds: Jamaica to
England to Ireland to France to Italy to Greece to Warsaw; bearing
fruit in the fields & vineyards of Industry, Science, Labor & Politics.
& the year, 1831 Charles Darwin (1809–1882) & Abraham Lincoln
(1809–1865), 2 2 score & 2 years old tide-turners to be, shove off:

Darwin aboard H.M.S. Beagle, sails for the Galapagos Islands, as
Lincoln on a flatboat, hauls cargo up & down the Mississippi. 1831.

"*I am in earnest —*" Garrison declares.
"*I will not equivocate —*
I will not excuse —
I will not retreat a single inch —" Hear

from the midst of the cloud
a thundering trumpet
heralding a lightning storm of change.
TA DOOM BOOM
BI-A BI-A BOOM
"*I WILL BE HEARD,*"
Garrison's salutation concludes.

But wait. See analogously, miraculously
the determined resurgence & re-formation
of the Black Face tradition,
(*black'face, n* . . .
       —a person made up as a Negro.
       —make-up used by performers of Negro
       roles, usually exaggerated for comic effect)
which, when fully cast in its reborn make up will
be baptized MINSTRELSY.

This new A-MERICAN MINSTRELSY will be hailed
the
       "*only original American Institution.*"
       The "*American National Opera.*"
We will
       see, the sweep & sway of MINSTRELSY's

notions where-ever A-

MERICANs gather &
manifest Uncle Sam's name. We will see these im-
pressions strike pay dirt. The main vein. The bonanza.
The Mother Lode. & the question we will ask is
Why? Why is MINSTRELSY, its form, content &
tenets, its doggerel dogma all the rage? & so
rapidly, so absolutely? Why is the
aspirant A-MERICAN consumer's pump so
primed? Their consumer's psyche so psyched, so set, so
tuned, so teed, keyed, groomed, geared, so inclined? So ready
& raring to hearken to, be taken by the
MINSTREL maelstrom? Why? the question is, is it?
What method, what manner of manipulation, what
means of misdirection sires this dark art's
popularity? What entreats, what attracts the
masses' asses to the seats?

& what about the
simultaneity of timing? A
coincidence you think? Happenstance, perchance? The
seemingly simultaneous geneses of
the antipodal factions of MINSTRELSY &
Radical Abolitionism. A freak astral
alignment? you wonder. A serendipitous
transpiration? Or, perhaps

(the cynical might
assert) a conspiratorial connivance; a con-
trivance; each side's fire fanned to fight the flames of
their opposite's philosophic extremes, UMPH! UMPH,
as they rally 'round, strike up the band & For-*Ward!*
ONE,

TA DOOM BOOM
2, for a long *March* into and through
the 1840s,

THREE, 4.

See, as in *Nocturne*
in Black and Gold: The Falling Rocket (James Abbott

McNeill Whistler, 1834–1903)
the rising through the billows, the bursting in air,
the showering down, on the housetops & the face
of the ground, like a holiday flare
illuminating the immigrating

TRAMP
tramp
TRAMP tramp of Europe's expelled & exported poor,
tired & wretched; refugee fleers from the
trampling hoof beats of the great horsemen 4: Famine,
Civil Strife, Death & War. Clippity clopp. See the
German, English, Irish, French, Welch fortune seekers
disembark on the golden shore. 1, 2, 3
million plus, strong & weak, seek wealth & sanctum. See
their rope-wrapped trunks, sacks, packs, baskets, parcels, boxes
& bundles. Smell the sea-salted reek of steerage
sickness, anxiety, desire, yearning &
bridges burning. Hear the babel of the *omnium*
gatherum: the bedlam: the din & clamor of
the cacophonous medley of dialects &
mother tongues. See the reception line. See the
émigrés first duty & right of passage: the
Ceremony of Translation at the Altar
of Custom(s), as in a lamb-like lockstep of
initiation, purification & re-
naming, *ONE*, 2, *THREE*, 4, they are shuffled & stamped
& shuffled, shuffled, shuffled, shuffled, shuffled &
stamped: bohunk, STAMP! polack, STAMP! frog, STAMP! paddy,
STAMP! kraut! kike! ruskie! & wop! *STAMP*! STAMP! *STAMP*!
STAMP! SHUFFLE & STAMP! STAMP! Hear them fore-warned:

"Lay down the burdensome baggage of your heritage,

your old hat habits, traditions, manners, ways &
mores & conform & be reformed in this more
Perfect Union, in order to belong, forget,
fit, as befits New Land outlanders longing to
be reconstituted in the hunky-dory,
Yankee-Doodle mold, according to Custom(s) &
the accepted conventions of Paradise Found
in A-MERICA the Bountiful.

"Hard work, Industrious Character, Thrift, Purpose,
Diligence, Temperance &," Tick Tock,
"Punctuality are the golden bricks paving
the Road to Virtue & A-MERICAN Success.
Further more," they're forewarned,
"for your own & the greater good,
before the sweet bandwagon bearing
'FREE WHITE PERSONS' stops & lets you ride, be on-lookers,
                                                    side-liners
(cluster with countrymen, brethren
& friends [i.e., one's own kind—of course], to avoid
friction or internal combustion)"
                            (& ah, Doodah
there is the ironic rub)
                        Hear them further forewarned,
"Construct & conduct yourselves according to local standards &
                                            customs.
To segregate, hyphenate,
pledge allegiance to, or align oneself with any
sect, circle, clique, or clan is separatist,
nationalistic, un A-MERICAN &
unfailingly to be avoided."
                        (Hear Hear!)
                                    &
a wise man hearing 1 word
understands 2,
        adds 2 to see that
            for

survival &
Hope's sake,
or a chance, or an opportunity, or the
likelihood, or possibility that fortune,
fate, destiny, Providence, or the gods, just might
conceivably, superveniently, perhaps, may-
be, on a gamble, or fluke, allow a toehold,
a foot in the door, a lucky break at a new
beginning t'ward one's uplifting by one's own boot-
straps.
      (Hah Hah.)

                   & like a litany, a prayer,
adjuration, invocation, or counting sheep,
they slump into a laborious sleep, mouthing, *"Hard
Work, Thrift, Purpose, Diligence, Industrious
Character, Temperance, Punctuality."*

                             Just
about then, as foresaid, Black Face Minstrelsy,

as if in a dream
or answered prayer,
rears its head.
Black Face, "a person made up as a Negro . . . *make-
up used by performers of Negro roles, usually
exaggerated for comic effect,"* this rooted,
persisting stir spurs non-blacks (for fun, profit or
psychic well-being) to blacken up, or down, &
parade *ONE*, 2, *THREE*, 4, aspects of *"negro
characteristics"* in public or private out-
lets (for fun, profit or psychic well-being.)

See
vulgarized re-tailed Minstrel appropriations
sold as authentications:
          "as composed and sung

by
them,"
the handbills & billboards say.
                          See the skin deep
imaginings of slave's peculiarities
(of togs & tongue) ripe for ridicule & re-
created for the recreation & infor-
mation of the new Yankee-Doodle common worker-
consumer Man. The aspirant All A-
                          MERICAN.

👉 Note: Not free from time. No, tethered to the new tempo of the
assembly line's rhythmic rush, but, & here's the thing, with free time,
aspiration time, time for the pursuit of the plucking of the oranges &
apples of the system, the fruit of the market place.

Read it as growth. Headway. Progress. See
Minstrels plumb the pith of the (so-called) "cherished
tradition" of (so-called) All A-
                          MERICAN values
& taste (so-called).
                          See Minstrels become The All A-
MERICAN Entertainment.
& more.
But, Dear Reader, if the above seems too harsh,
too Afrocentric'ly judgmental, too
conspiratorial in nature, & we seem't've
strayed from the straight path (Hah Hah doo-Derrida-dah)
perhaps to find our way we must enter into
the gloomy wood & slippery slopes of Theory,
dearie.
        In that case, consider the notion &
motion of Minstrelsy as some do, as merely
the muddled huddle's wistful, Proustian lament
for less progressive things past, the less hectic
hugger mugger of pre-Industrial innocence.
A tentative toe dipped testingly in the

tranquil river of nostalgia, they posit. Only
this & nothing more, surely nothing with racial
intent they implore. A cigar is just a stogie,
a show is just a show. (Ho Ho!)

On the other
hand, as you consider that, consider this:
Minstrelsy as white magic liturgy & new
blue-collar voodoo; some serious doo-doo.

(Hang
on now, the irony gets as thick through here as
Sambo's lips or the woolly brambles on his
nappy noggin.)

CHAPTER 3

 A Brief Passage on the Emergence of

the Democratic Party, Daddy Rice,

Uncle Sam, Indians & "Discovery"

1832

Make a note. Just about now, 1832, the Democratic Party invents itself; Samuel F. B. Morse begins work on an electric telegraph; the Supreme Court grants the U.S. exclusive rule over all Indians & their lands; *"A-merica,"* the patriotic anthem, Umph Umph, is written to the tune of *"God Save the Queen,"* Umph Umph; the New England Anti-Slavery Society is formed in Boston. & T. D. (Thomas Danforth) Rice (1808–1860) debuts his Jim Crow cameos at Louisville, Kentucky's City Theatre, bedecked in a swallow-tail sky-colored coat, & in a parody of the stage Yankee, parti-colored trousers striped red, white & blue. Beneath his star-banded high hat Rice's face is blackened. 20 encores are alleged. (Much as Stephen Foster before him, acquired his *"Knowledge"* of negroes' ways & means, Rice later brags he, *"studied the Negro character on Southern plantations."*

E pluribus unum,

Rice

among the dark & lowly, Doodah,

"discovers" his

        "song"

Doodah Daa

Discovers.

"*Hummmmmm —*" to quote the Kingfish. No, not Huey Pierce Long (1893–1935). Demagogue whose song & dance was "*Share the Wealth,*" as he did his corn pone Doodah behind the mask of a politician, Louisiana style. No, I mean *The* Kingfish, George Stevens. No, not that George Stevens (1904–1975), film director of *A Place in the Sun* & *Giant*, who in the 1950s said no to movie mogul Cecil B. DeMille's demand for loyalty oaths from members of the director's guild & was a man before the HUAC. I mean George Kingfish Stevens (created 1928 on a Chicago radio station), Kingfish of the Mystic Knights of the Sea Lodge. Born a white, blackened faced radio minstrel, on the *Amos 'n' Andy Show* (whose theme was the "Perfect Song," which was written for *The Birth of a Nation*) & resurrected with a later life, 1951–1953, on TV portrayed by Harry Roscoe "Tim" Moore (1887–1958), who made his way with a turn-about and wheel-about as a seller of cure-all potions; carnival *"geek"*; *"native"* Hawaiian tour guide; stable fly-shooer; fight manager; jockey; boxer, a.k.a. *"Young Klondike"*; one-man *Uncle Tom's Cabin* portraying Simon Legree *&* Uncle Tom, with half his face made up with white chalk; partner of Mantan Moreland; star of Oscar Michaeux's 1931 film *Darktown*; several times guest on Ed Sullivan's *Toast of the Town*; & lead actor on the aforementioned *Amos 'n' Andy* till the NAACP finally had their say & got their way: "Why the Amos 'n' Andy TV Show Should Be Taken Off the Air," *NAACP Bulletin, August 15, 1951.* *"1. It intends to strengthen the conclusion among uninformed and prejudiced people that Negroes are inferior, lazy, dumb and dishonest. 2. Every character in this one and only TV show with an all Negro cast is either a clown or a crook. 3. Negro doctors are shown as quacks and thieves. 4. Negro lawyers are shown as slippery cowards, ignorant of their profession and without ethics. 5. Negro Women are shown as cackling, screaming shrews, in big mouthed close-ups, using street slang, just short of vulgarity. 6. All Negroes are shown as dodging work of any kind. 7. Millions of white Americans see this Amos 'n' Andy picture of Negroes and think the entire race is the same."* & laid the whole holy mackerel mess to rest. Him. That Kingfish. *"Humm —"* he'd say, stroking his chin, his wily eyes turned heaven-ward as he mused on the colonialist's misfunction of the lexicon, or vamped while "conjecturat'n'" on the turns & "numerat'n'" on the twists of

his next colonialist-like scam, *discovered* a scheme to *claim* the natural
possessions & share the wealth of Brother Andy, a.k.a. Andrew H.
Brown.

"Discovers" is linked in history books with names
acclaimed heroic. Pictured as square-jawed, straight-backed,
steely eyed, living verbs; first, the insinuation
is, of humankind to behold, to find some site,
cradle or pinnacle superb. Being the first —
the insinuation is — the measure of the
import of their *"discovery."* That they simply
happened upon, or were guided to some exotic
place, or source, or crest abroad — if you think about it —
is less reason to applaud said so-called
"discoverers" claiming & renaming for
mother country or monarch, a point, root or
pinnacle whose existence or location, he,
as an outsider — from the natives' point of view —
deserves no place in the discoverer's
hierarchical queue.

&/so, in concert with
the Kingfish, one must *"Hummm"* at the verity of
"discovers" being linked to many of the
instances & events with which it is connected.
As, for instance, blue eyed, prematurely graying redhead Christopher
Columbus (1451–1506), a.k.a. Cristoforo Colombo, a.k.a. Cristobal
Colon, a.k.a. Xpisto Ferens (Bearer of Christ), Italian-Spanish
navigator, descendant of weavers & self proclaimed *"Ambassador of
God,"* who through a series of miscalculations *"discovers"* the New
World, then thinks he *"discovers"* a river running from Biblical Eden.
Columbus, a.k.a. Colombo, a.k.a. Colon, writes, *"I discovered a great
many islands inhabited by people without number: and of them all I have taken
possession on behalf of Their Highnesses by proclamation and with the royal
flag extended, and I was not opposed."* Writes, the inhabitants were *"so
guileless and generous with what they have that one would not believe it with
out seeing it."* Writes, *"They did not know any sect or idolatry, except that*

they all believe that power and goodness abide in heaven. Indeed, they believed very firmly that I with these ships and people came from heaven. . . . They are the most faint-hearted people in the world." Thinks: *"A paradise on Earth."* Claims it, names it (San Salvador) *"Holy Savior"* (nudge nudge). Writes, *"The island offers no danger . . . as long as . . . [we] know how to govern it."* Preceding *"The Admiral"* as he also addressed himself. (There was a Saint Christopher from the 3rd century. A giant who became a Christian & later a martyr who carried travelers across the rivers.)

On Christmas day, 1499, a heavenly voice, tells the "discoverer" who feared that lurking there were beheading, blood-drinking men, some 1-eyed & some with dogs' snouts & possibly giants about, *"Be not afraid, nor fear. I will provide for all."* This heavenly assurance plus Columbus' contract with Their Highnesses ceding him 10% of all "treasure found" stood him in good stead. He wrote, *"Their Highnesses can see that I will give them as much gold as they may need. . . . Also spices and cotton, as much as Their Highnesses order me to load . . . and as many slaves as they order loaded. . . . Eternal be God our Lord, who grants, to all those who walk in His path, victories over things that appear impossible."* & that & the rest, Doodah, as they say, is his story, & the turned-around, watered-down history. Note the irony. (Nudge nudge.)

"Discovers" 's been defined as, *"To be the first
to find out, see, or know about."* No, Chris — no points
there. No dice for you either, Rice. The Countrymen,
the natives, the local yokels, knew — where they were
& who. So knew no credit are you due; that
"discovering" wasn't real, no thrill, no big deal.
No cause for renown because you'd just happened 'pon them
while stumbling 'roun'.

It's just as with David Livingstone (1813–1873), Scottish doctor & missionary, castigator of Arab &

Portuguese slave trading, *"discovering"* the Zambezi River, Victoria Falls, & Lakes Ngami, Nyasa, Chilwa & Bangweulu, & being hailed as *"one of the greatest modern African explorers."* (Nudge nudge.)

 Aside: & on the docks & in the basements of the Brit Museum crates of crafts & curios pile up like props in Charles Foster Kane's gated Xanadu awaiting clerks & pedagogues to sort & order for shelving, display or flame. Livingstone dies, Doodah, seeking the source of the Nile. & that, as they say, is his-story.

Just as with Rice, *"discovering his song."* Note the irony. (Nudge nudge.)

Like a motherless, lap-snuggled child nuzzling at
the mammy-like bosom, Rice, a.k.a. *"Daddy"*
Rice, suckles the milk of Inspiration from the
nourishing tit of black being. & that & the
rest, as they say, is his story. Not to be confused,
for our purposes with history. Rice's "act,"

his "discovery," as legend has it, that:
   "Wheel about,
   turn about,
   do just
   so,
   & every time I wheel about,
   I jump Jim Crow,"

is, in substance, carriage, choreography
& dialect *"assumed"* (legend assumes) from some
stable slave's ditty & dance, Doodah. Its namesake
stage musical debuts in Louisville, Kentuck'.
Hailed with a hearty Ha Ha & a Hip-Hip Hippidy
Doodah, is an instant hit! But not unheard of.
No anomaly. Not even novel in terms
of unusual, different, or strikingly new.
White A-MERICANs doing *"traditional"*
darkened faced mis-representations go back, way
back, as far back we've foresaid as the 17 hundreds.

ASIDES, SERIES 1
Containing numerous asides on minstrelsy-like occurrences in the American
Revolution, and passing, Crispus Attucks, the "negro," and stock stereotypes.

Return with us now to those thrilling days of yesteryear.
Recall the so-called Boston Tea Party? A prelude to the A-
MERICAN Revolution, that conflict between jolly old United
Kingdom imperialists, seeking taxation & benefits from the patrician
land-grabbing culprit's proceeds, gleaned while preaching piety &
sacking & dispatching the land's first citizens. The business of A-
MERICA being foremost & after all, business.

Preparing for their act of rebellion costumed
patriots, short on the courage of their over-taxed
convictions, color (nudge nudge) their *"face and hands*
with cold dust," to quote a participant. It is
hoped that their British critics suspend their disbelief
& assume the disguises & renegade
performance to be authored & enacted by
"red skins"—like the nudging & budging forth of brother

Attucks? — &, if there's to be retribution for
their taxed tea's redistribution, those crafty
savages (mini ha ha) 'll be the ones The Crown'll
dump their persecution upon. (This, an early
instance of A-MERICAN whites exploiting
"passing," i.e., forging beyond the pale [nudge nudge].
"Passing" is the clandestine crossing of a
"color line." *"Passing"* is, for the colonists, as
with the light-skinned blacks able to *"pass"* the other
way, a radical, even revolutionary
[nudge nudge] racial act.)

But concerning the Boston Tea Party & the
business of the cold dust-red skin ruse, one wonders
about the logic there, if logic plays any
part in it. Or is it simply a proclivity
toward subliminal minstrelsy, triggered by
the err of their imagined representation,
their lionization of blacks & Natives'
rebellious spirit? An unconscious slipping
across the line between protest & awed, but
forbidden, admiration? One wonders, that's all.

But, as revolutionary times call for
revolutionary acts & actors, escaped
slave, dock-worker & patriot Crispus Attucks
(c. 1723–1770),
to a chorus of drums, chants & church chimes, rebukes
his fellows' fears & rocks George the Second's world,
by baptizing the idea of rebellion in
his blood when he, *"a Molatto Fellow, about
. . . 6 Feet two Inches height, short curl'd Hair,
his Knees nearer together than common,"* & toting *"a
large cordwood stick,"* steps forth, following fisticuffs
& a snowball attack against bayonets &
muskets, from *"a motley rabble of saucy boys,
negroes and mulattoes, Irish teagues & outlandish*

jack tarrs," to quote John Adams (1735–
1826), defense attorney for the Redcoats,
signatory to the Declaration of
Independence & 2nd President
of the United States of A-MERICA.
A redcoat's musket ball barks. Bites. Barks. Bites.
Attucks falls, fatally, to the herringbone-patterned
brick. 2 lead balls to the breast. 11 others,
dead or wounded, follow his lead.

One wonders if it was all Attucks' notion; a rash, impassioned action
of a brash brawler's anti-British zeal; or, if he was perhaps ill-advised;
budged forward (nudge nudge) cued by some hang-back patriot,
some petty-player shunning the spot-light's heat by letting this dark
stand-in, of mingled descent — part Wampanoag, a.k.a. Natick,
Massachusetts, or Pokanoket part A-MERICAN-African — strut to
center stage & star (nudge nudge) as Premier Martyr in the Boston
Massacre: Act I, Scene I of the rebellious drama, the A-MERICAN
Revolution. Or, was it a chance crossing of a road, illuminated, of a
sudden, in history's headlights? Attucks, *"the first to defy, and the first to
die,"* means, in Natick, *"deer."*

👉 Aside: The Wampanoags were the 1st Natives met by the
Pilgrims upon landing at Plymouth. *"We,"* American activist Malcolm
X (1925–1965) said, *"didn't land on Plymouth Rock. . . . Plymouth rock
landed on us!"* Twas the turkey & corn brung by the Wampanoags to
help the ungrateful immigrant Pilgrims through the winter. In turn
they were given firewater & land-ceding treaties to sign. Protesters
were slaughtered, enslaved, stripped of their tribal identity & exiled.
Thanksgiving Day commemorates the experience. Doodah.

👉 Aside: In that war's early battles at Lexington & Concord 10
blacks die; at Bunker Hill, Salem Poor, a black, leads & fights with
particular distinction, as do 25,000 other blacks who throughout that
war fight for their notion of freedom.

👉 Aside: In the official report, those who fell with Attucks, all
white, had their names preceded by *"Mr."* Attucks did not.

The Boston Massacre by Paul Revere

Attucks was portrayed in an engraving by Paul Revere (c. 1734–1818), American *silversmith* and *patriot*, as a white man.

☞ Aside: Was Mr. William Warren who fired the fatal shots. Warren & the other 8 of His Majesty's soldiers of the 29th Regiment were defended by John Adams. Among their victims were a chance amassing of 20 or 30 so-called outside agitators, including a rope maker, ships mate & apprentice joiner. *"If this was not an unlawful assembly, there never was one in the world,"* Adams argued, & called Attucks, *"a stout man" with a 20 year old 10 Pounds bounty on his head for escape from slavery, & (tossing a race card in the pot?),* Adams said, *"whose very looks was enough to terrify any person,"* & *"To whose mad behavior . . . the dreadful carnage of that night is chiefly to be ascribed."*

Well, *"what a revoltin' development that [was],"* to quote Chester A. Riley, Irish American riveter, postwar, blue-collar, everyman (1943–1951) resident of NBC Radio-land & 1953–1958 NBC television. The judicial system agreed. The Red Coats were acquitted. Self-defense.

☞ Aside: In 1781 the Brits, crying uncle, face the music: *"Yankee Doodle,"* played with *Oompah!* by boasting A-MERICANs.

☞ Aside: Yankee-Doodle was intended as a signification by the British. *"Doodle"* dates back to a Low German word: fool. Yankees, in (nudge nudge) an about face, turn it into a popular fife & drum ditty (Note the irony) to the tune of a fine old English melody.

As they strike colors, pack their Union Jack & sail away, *"The World Turned Upside Down"* is played by the defeated Brits' own martial band, & 2, *THREE,* 4, &/so the curtain falls on the Pax Britannica colonization of A-MERICA.

☞ Aside: In the newly free & independent A-MERICAN states, neither the news, nor spirit, nor meaning of Liberty reach the owners of humans not conceived as equal. Slavery in notion & name remain intact. Note the irony. (Nudge nudge.)

Or,

does the A-MERICAN notion of Black Face
"a person made up as a Negro . . . make-up used
by performers of Negro roles, usually exaggerated for comic effect"
loom not from a free black, like Attucks, but from in-
sightful white performers made up as Southern negroes
summoned to amuse Massa & Missy's
plantation party guests during slavery,
that long-running drama from the days of our
Colonial lives?

 Aside: How like the New Nation's notions of its New Negro.

Laugh bait in & of themselves, these *others*, are plucked
from the piles of various Old Country's stock-types.
To cite a couple more: whiskered German kooks called Hans,
& whiskied Irish loons tagged Paddy.

Fair or not,
all foreigners are fair game, & when liberally
translated ease easily into the
Dramatis Personae of the A-MERICAN negro.

The A-MERICAN negro. The A-MERICAN negro is an invention.

In-ven-tion:
"A mental fabrication, especially a false-hood." The *A-MERICAN Negro is an*
invention. In-ven-tion: "A new device, method, or process developed from study
and experimentation." The A-MERI-CAN negro is an invention.
In-ven-tion: *"A discovery, a finding."* (Nudge nudge) The A-MERICAN
negro is an invention.
ne-gro: *"see [NEGER & NIGGER.] An individual (esp. a male) belonging*
to the African race of mankind, which is distinguished by a black skin, black

wooly hair, flat nose and thick protruding lips."
The A-MERICAN negro, a non-human being contrived to fit a need,
has a patent date of 1619. Therefore the A-MERICAN Negro is 157
years older than A-MERICA, invented in 1776. The negro, Ambrose
Bierce (1842–1914?) defines it in his *Devil's Dictionary* as, *"The piece
de resistance in the American political problem."* The A-MERICAN negro
is an invention. *"A nigger,"* anonymous said, *"is a negro out of sight of a
white man."* In musical parlance an in-ven-tion is, *A short composition
developing a single theme contrapuntally.* (Author's emphasis. I.e., single
theme: like a stereotype.) *"A conventional, formulaic, and oversimplified
conception, opinion, or image."*
The A-MERICAN negro is an invention.

Aside: A thing, at best, is but a thing: mask, grass, cigar, gold
bar, negro, or a middle class. A thing. Alone, it lacks merit, beauty,
message or consequence. Is an it. An *it* in need of the greed of mores,
guilds, psyche, or Grace, in need of the edge of consensus, or force of
arms to confer it its worth. It then becomes Precious, Prized. Proto-
type. The Standard, even. &/so, alas, it is with these inventions: the
negro. A-MERICA. The middle class. & blackened-faced minstrels.

*ASIDES Series 2
Containing a follow-up on discoverers, American Minstrelsy and its European
antecedent, buckras, hence, niggardly, class, the Blues again, and dark matter.*

&/so,

behold the blackened faced white explorers venturing
into the territory of satiric
traditions & finding an A-MERICAN form
to be called MINSTRELSY. See the makers of this
new found fun, their black masks
(**mask·ing** [màs'kîng] *noun*
        Physiology. The concealment or screening of one sensory
process or sensation by another.)
cloaking their visages
like visors, or *"vizards,"* in the Bard's way of saying,

hiding the rugged ruthlessness of their thick
thudding ambition as they jest & prance.

&/so,
just as white indentured servants precede the black enslaved
as gentry's slogs & whipping boys, imported
blackened faced white figures precede A-MERICAN
Minstrel notions of the folks as neutered ciphers
& selfless fools.

Aside: Fool, in point of fact as serendipity, irony or common
sense would have it, even in its 13th century English origins is rooted
in the Latin word *follies* meaning wind-bloated bag or big old bellows-
like ball.

Aside: 17th Century Africans upon meeting Europeans read
their bluster, their insular insolence, their brass neck pride of
presumption & cast a wide conceptual & signifying net. They typed
them odd-balls; christen them buckras. In their accounts to the public
back home, the invaders, with Explorer stenciled on their letterhead,
acknowledged, *"buckra,"* *"belonging or pertaining to the white man; term
originating in Africa."*
but,
in their folly of the fluffing of their own feathers & through denial,
failure, or refusal, the trespassers did not associate buckra with stiff,
starched, or stuck up, as from buckram, *"a course cotton, hemp, or linen
cloth, stuffed with glue . . . used in garments to keep them in the form intended."*

Aside: On notions of doodles & fools, & who's whose, this time
quoting F. Scott Fitzgerald, *"jazz age"* spokesman (nudge nudge)
(1896–1940), *"When people are taken out of their depths, they lose their
heads, no matter how charming a bluff they may put up."*

Nor, in their arrogance, affectation, artifice & sneering sanctimony do
the encroachers make the buckra connection to *"also men in buckram:
some-times proverbially non-existent persons . . ."* *". . . to pad or stiffen with
buckram; to give to false appearance of strength."*

Indeed, in their quest for booty, souls & facts, the explorers &
discoverers sent thither, are, whether naive or nefarious, self-captives
of their pious, bloated, windbag hum-buggery, & upon being greeted
by *griots*, their host's holders of the royal post of Conservators of
History & Chief Diplomats, these infringers, for that is what they
are, & not paled gods poured from heaven like manna, nor civilized
saviors guided by Providence; they were trespassers, interlopers,
buckras, traveling on the European plan (nudge nudge) who mistake
the story-keepers for fiddlers, fools, no better than buffoons.

Aside: **Griot**, or **Djalli** (Ha-Ha) is a *West African poet*, a praise
singer who is a repository of the wisdom and the history of his people.

Aside: An instrument the *griots* or *djallis* played, & the nimble,
quick-footed dance done to it was the *bambazo*. Think'st there's a
connection to bamboozle, meaning both to banter & to sham, which
surfaced in English writing a few years after the establishment of
British slave trade in Africa? If there's any connection, makes you
wonder, again, who was fooling who? Huh?

Aside: Katherine Anne Porter (1890–1980), Amer. novelist,
author of (nudge nudge) *Ship of Fools*, countering or concurring notes,
"A cultivated style would be like a mask. Everybody knows it's a
mask, and sooner or later, you show yourself as someone who could
not afford to show himself, and so created a style. You work, and
develop yourself; your style is an emanation of your own being."

mask·ing (màs'kîng) *noun*
1. *Physiology*. The concealment or screening of one sensory process or
sensation by another.

& men, someone must have noted, who mistake wise men for fools
are themselves fools. &/so it is with these self defined *"explorers,"* these
stiff upper lip & stuffed shirt & starched collared *"discoverers,"* who
while in the puffery of their hubris, in the presence of philosopher
praise-singers & wits, are capable only of exploring with pride-
blinded eyes; of perceiving only with insolence-deafened ears;
discerning no more of, or from, these living bridges between past &

future, ancestors & descendants, than a donkey divines from long
division.

&/so, the insights/perceptions, the deeply held prejudgments reduce
their possibility to simply see or say what is & then translate it for
their stay-at-home audience without addled patter. This, for example,
from *The Dictionary of Phrase and Fable* by E. Cobham Brewer (1894)

*"BUCKRA Superior, excellent. That's buckra. A buckra coat is a smart coat;
a buckra man, a man of consequence." "This word among the West Indians
does the service of burra among the Anglo-Indians: as burra saib (great major,
i.e., white man), burra khana (a magnificent dinner)."* (Blowing smoke up
one's own arse with the billows of one's own blustering spin)

&/so it comes down to *Webster's Dictionary of the English Language
Unabridged Deluxe Edition* (c) 1977, *"Master,"* as
*"a white. Belonging or pertaining to the white man;
hence, good & strong . . .*

". . . hence, good & strong."
"pertaining to the white man;
hence,
        good & strong."

Were you dozing just now? Or did
you dig it? Did you note the flip flop doodle?
The verbal bamboozle. The reversal,
the social, historical & psychological somersault
of so-called logic:
        "pertaining to the white man;
        hence,
        good & strong."

Just
whose
"hence"
is that?

Which of *Webster's Dictionary of the English Language Unabridged Deluxe
Edition* (c) 1977's
minions made that leap?
Was't a hurdle of folly
or faith, or a stealthful step crept surreptitiously
while no eye spied? a tree's silent fall in an un-
manned forest? a strident, uncontested, steering committee stride
taken without debate? a Board proclamation; a CEO declaration;
an edict from an even Higher Authority,
or a presumed truth held self evident?
The reliable, the undeniable. The
Imperialistic Ying & Yangian Principle:
 "White
 + Might =
 Right";
Hence:
adv. 1.a. For this reason; therefore. b. From this source.
2. From this time; from now. 3.a. From this place; away from here.
b. From this life, the *American Heritage Dictionary* tells us,

hence
it's easy inclusion to the exclusion of
all other conclusions. Perhaps, in all innocence
no switcheroo, no dyslexic daring-do was
meant, no message intended sent, no sleight of hand,
no deliberate twist in the transcribing was
intended t'ward the offended, & the about face
(nudge nudge) was inadvertent.
Accidents do happen, after all.
No one can deny that. (But, where's the
logic in it?) & if there is, then whose?

In any case, in the African's sense of it
(tho many would forget over time),
                                        buckra,
meaning *"so-so"* at best, is a notion secreted
o'er the sea & is, as a savored cultural holding,

(tho many would forget over time) as
crucial a part of that wretched trek as memories
of home, or the wind that whipped them to that fearsome foreign shore.
&/so,
buckra, a covert signifying
snub in the minds of the newly enslaved, then so
new in it till they still knew who they truly were
(tho many would forget over time), so that at
the onset of blackened-faced minstrelsy, their
perception of buckra as penurious,
pernicious, avaricious, niggardly
was still a shield against the *"hence"*; knew
(tho many would forget over time) *"hence"* was in fact not a fact,
not scripture, not Truth, but just a theory, a
psychological & system-supporting wish,
wrapped in the security blanket of an art form,
'cause their enslavers sensed as German social philosopher
Friedrich Engels (1820
–1895) would note, quote *"An ounce of action is
worth a ton of theory,"* unquote, is what he wrote,
so began peddling—like wolf tickets, or all-
purpose snake oil, a whitening & brightening
notion-potion to get out the grit & grime that
history, left behind; knew (but many would forget
over time) it wasn't *"hence"* that was the secret
ingredient of the buckra business, but that
the business of A-MERICAN buckra business
was ju ju doo-doo, concocted to build, albeit
bleached, a dream & a genre on, but, to its core,
penurious, pernicious, avaricious &
niggardly ne'er the less.

See: *nig-gard-ly, adv., 1. like or characteristic of a niggard; covetous or
avaricious; parsimonious; stingy; miserly. Of obscure etymology* O.E.D.
claims, citing a Chaucer usage circa 1374. Nigger, on the other hand,
1. a negro in everyday speech with contemptuous connotations, is first cited in
1786.

Aside: By the by, the claim from Britain's latter day defenders, foisterers of the post imperial imperialistic faith is: *"It was class."* *"Class,"* they preach, attempt to teach. *"Class! Was our game. Simply a sense of Pageantry & Place, all in upper case. If we're guilty, & we've no reason to be, but if we're guilty at all, if that's your call, then Classism, a love of parades & tradition, order & erudition was our empyreal sin. We never considered our conquered's color of skin but their place on the map. We're innocent as lambs of the racism rap. It was their manner, & their means, not (necessarily primarily) their genes."*

&/so (tho many would forget over time)
67 years after the creation of the
A-MERICAN negro, & 412
years post O.E.D.'s citing of *niggardly*,
turns out,

    doodah, The whole niggardly notion was
first about whites; about some dark matter 'mongst themselves; some
inner-tribal malevolence
churning at the heart of their *own* darkness, &
only secondarily, after-the-fact-ly,
by-the-by-ly, to do with the varicolored
colonial subjects being slowly reformed
like volatile decomposing organic matter
beneath layers of massive, unrelenting
Imperialistic pressure. Puts another
face on it, huh?

Aside: Blackface, like nigger, like coal, like the blues
is the deep dark matter,
formed when volatile organic substance
slowly breaks down, slowly
breaks down beneath massive layers
of unrelenting pressure.
(Nudge
nudge.) See,
the highest quality Blackface, as with nigger,
as with coal,

as with the blues,
is created under the conditions
of greatest stress &
mined by workers with blackened faces,
whose gig is to dig
down deep, dig
down deep to
get it. Get
it. &
as we put our minds right on it,
remember their products' properties
of coal & the blues:
heat & energy — & how
their residue blackens (nudge
nudge) every-
thing exposed
to them.

&/so among their own race
the buckras: the low' classed, the landless whites,
the lesser, the squatters, strangers, square pegs,
scabs, the misfits, are recast & blackened down so A-
MERICANs can recognize these staple
European common worker-consumer
"nigger" sorts in the A-MERICAN scheme of things.
Said simply, these white buckras are representation,
without taxation to the pauper's purse of A-
MERICAN appreciation & discrimination.
They're the notion of insignificant others;
the virtue-less lot representing what those (in
their own minds) of vital significance, are not.
Hold on now as we continue our minefield maneuvers
through the muzzy mesh & maze of semantics &
etymological antics.
& as we meander forth, if you'll be so kind,
keep this question in mind, Could it be that the whole racial/
cultural industry, including minstrelsy & black face

& all that, isn't really about race a'tall,
but an American Museum of the whispers
& echoes of internal dark matters that exhibits themselves
first as inner-tribal anxieties?
That the new sensation of the freakish blackened face mask
they jostle & bump to witness is but the visible form
of the dark matter of their own questions
& attempts at transference. Doodah.

Aside: Back to Thomas "Daddy" Rice for a moment, if we
may. Conventional scholarship has long assumed & often affirmed,
believed, championed, decreed, embraced, featured, granted, hailed,
identified Rice as the initial, the jump start, the kickoff, *le premier*,
mouth, nascent, overture, prelude, the rising of the curtain of
blackened-faced white MINSTRELSY. That, Dear Reader, as we
see, or will come to
    know,
  ain't necessarily, or
even, no-wise, so.

CHAPTER

 Treats of Minstrels and Minstrelsy,

Invention of the Common Man,

the Jacksonian Era, and

Indians Conceding Their Lands

Perhaps the confusion comes
with the use of "MINSTRELS" & "MINSTRELSY"
in an A-MERICAN framework.

For Minstrel the O.E.D. compact 1971 edition lists 22 forms of the
word.
Among its definitions: *"a servant having a special function."*
Minstrelsy has 32 listed forms. It is variously defined as:
*"1. The art, occupation, or practice of a minstrel; the practice of playing and
singing. . . . 2. A body of minstrels; an assemblage or gathering of minstrels. In
early use (i.e. down to the end of the 16th c.), a general designation for anyone
whose profession was to entertain his patrons with singing, music, and story-
telling, or with buffoonery or juggling."*
Further down we get:
"The use of the word in romantic poetry and fiction has so coloured (nudge
nudge) *its meaning that the application to a mere jester, mountebank, or
conjuror, originally common, would now seem inappropriate."*
(Hear Hear.) Seems what comes around has been around before,
disguised or otherwise, fair of face or
foul. 18 Hundreds' solo actors doing gnarled
but "good natured" BLACK FACE notions

of the behavioral debilities of everyday
negroes, foreigners, dolts & strangers, are predated
in dances & doings by Jolly Ol' England's
stage-staple clowns billed as *"rustics"* & *"fools."*
Seems they were common as whale oil & candle wax.

&/

so, the new aspirant A-MERICANs in desperate search
of some thing that will closet Old Country skeletons
& open Future's door, "Some thing that will set our
sodden souls & lowly asses free at least, free,
at least, God Bless A-MERICA, free at least from
the feudal whims & polish of the Imperial
Highfalutin; so it ain't blood, nor manor, nor
manners, nor who (or what) we know, but plain & simply, what
we have of what's on the market that counts: be-
longings to fill new leisure time & sate new
leisure love for the fresh, the flesh, the up-to-the-
minute, the amusements, the hot commodity
diversions & creature conveniences, conceived
in Liberty & dedicated to the
proposition that access to the consumables
hatched for us
(tomorrow's Mister & Missus
Average Joe & Janie Doe),
is the real all A-
MERICAN ideal of Harmony, Order,
Fairness, Justice & Equality."

This during the so-called Jacksonian era (1829–1837) of the so-
called dawn of the invention of the so-called A-MERICAN Common
man. The worker consumer. What happens is the upper crust play
the class card & the aspiring *nouveau populi* with the first-raters'

sanction take a step forward, widening the gap between them, & it's the immigrants & blacks who remain stragglers, 3, 4, in the parade of humankind. Andrew Jackson (1767–1845). Democrat. Major General. 7th U.S. President. Also on his CV are an inventory of horse whippings, canings, shootings. Jackson, with a trigger finger quick as his temper, fights many *"Code Duello,"* so-called affairs of honor (his & his wife's) according to the code of the so-called Southern gentleman. He is dubbed *"the first bigamist president,"* by some who knew him, a *"worthless, drunken, black-guard scoundrel"* by others; *"the Hero of New Orleans"* by others; *"the Gin'ral"* or *"Old Hickory"* by his men; & *"one of the people"* by the friendly Press. He is a life-long drooler, with chronic hives & an abscessed bullet wound that reeks to high heaven. Jackson, Old Hickory/one of the people, Humph, says, *"One man with courage makes a majority"* & measures his mandate for the redskins' removal from their territory—his 1813 victor against the Creek at the Battle of Horseshoe Bend, gaining 23 million acres of their land for A-MERICA;

2, 3, 4,

"Old Hickory/one of the people," Humph

—by the mood of the country, a policy practiced by Presidents Jefferson, Monroe & J. Q. Adams before him. A-MERICANs, after all, feared for their National Security, after all, with all those Choctaw, Chickasaw, Chehaw, Chippewa, Kickapoo, Creek & Cherokee & all, led by Chiefs Bowlegs & Hopony, Big Warrior, Dragging Canoe, Bloody Fellow, Black Fox, Black Hawk, Mad Wolf, Little Warrior & the like, &, like after all, how long could reasonable people, of whom *"Old Hickory"* was one, Humph, be expected to tolerate the intolerable? How long? How long? So, he defied the Supreme Court & removed the Cherokee from their Georgia land;

2, 3, 4,

"Old Hickory/one of the people," Humph, 1814 war victory in the Battle of New Orleans, 2 weeks after the war was over;

3, 4,

Humph, Louisiana slaves were impressed into Jackson's army to fight on A-MERICA's side. The property fought like men. *"Old Hickory/one of the people,"* Humph, 1818 victor against the Florida

Seminoles & their black supporters & later bought the rest of the state for A-MERICA;

2, 3, 4

"Old Hickory/one of the people," Humph, of Scotch-Irish (Protestant) parents of no wealth, orphaned at 14, raised by slaveholder uncle & endowed with great connections;

2, 3, 4,

"Old Hickory/one of the people," Humph, 1st to use federal troops against labor;

2, 3, 4,

"Old Hickory/one of the people," *"Great Father,"* practitioner of the scorched earth policy on some of his Indian children who failed to *"remove,"* i.e., cede their land. Humph, *"Old Hickory/one of the people"* then sanctioned the invasion of Spanish Florida to destroy Ft. Negro housing hundreds of barbarous "negroe" runaway *"Banditti,"* *"enticed away from the service of their masters."*

"Old Hickory/one of the people," Humph, who of his 1834 inauguration it is said, *"the reign of the Mob seemed triumphant,"* as cronies & patronage seekers stamped, stamped, stamped (nudge nudge), through the official D.C. residence, the "President's Palace" & on through the 1830s, Humph,

2, 3, 4,

Was Irish-born James Hoban (1762?–1831), owner of 9 slaves, concocted the notion of a President's Palace, built 1792 to 1799 by immigrant & slave labor. Its face singed sooty black by British military arsonists in 1812, was whitewashed to restore its dignity. Was T. Roosevelt named it the White House in 1901 & has since remained.

CHAPTER

5

 The Middle Passage
P. T. Barnum, History as Entertainment
in Multi Voices

1835–1842

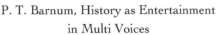

But back to the 1830s: '35, specifically, nearing the end of the
Jacksonian era. The aforementioned abolitionist Garrison at the
end of a pro-slavery mob's rope, is dragged, half naked, over Boston
cobblestones. A pattern emerges: abolitionists scold, theorize,
sermonize, BLACK FACE MINSTRELS finding their form & way,
act. Entertain. That same year, 1835, the U.S. cedes the Florida
Seminole's land. Under Osceola's leadership the Seminoles & their
black slaves exterminate 103 insurgent U.S. troops. Osceola is killed
after a 2 year guerrilla war. The final solution to the problem, his
people's extermination, takes a couple more years.

That same year, 1835, Phineas Taylor Barnum, *"P.T."*
(1810–1891), buys a black woman.
One Joice Heth. She looks like an Egyptian mummy.
She, it was claimed, had been nurse & breast feeder to
Washington, George (1732–1799),
when the big daddy of his country to be was her *dear
little George* was he. Heth,

THE GREATEST
NATURAL & *NATIONAL*
CURIOSITY
IN THE WORLD

AGE OF 160 YEARS

a slave, becomes the main attraction in Barnum's first show business
undertaking.

"Humbug," critics claimed.
When she dies next year it is claimed she, Joice Heth, *"is only 70-*
some-odd."
Sadder but richer, Barnum's meager freak fare, gathering no loss,
rolls on.

Just about then
       (still in the 1830s), buoyed
by the up-beat down-beat, a-marching
ONE, 2, THREE,
4,
     Hi-Ho-Hi-Ho, seeking inroads & a place
in the sum, the aspirant immigrant A-
MERICANs go, *"strong brawn'd,"* as Walt Whitman
(1819–1892), poet, nurse,
nomad, sage, an eyewitness, calls them, off on their
"journey-work"
       (the good gray poet again), off to
the stalls, mills, mines, carts, railbeds, docks & shops,
whistling *Stars and Stripes Forever*, clippity *THREE,*
4! clopp! while chasing the common wage,

&, when, from the ranks of workmen a body of
whites (naturalized or aspiring) meets a
body of free &/or enslaved blacks to heft, heave
& ho, supplying the wants & demands of A-
MERICA's consumers, there is,

to hear the alarmed
elite relate it — a mongrel commingling of
Pandora's boxfuls of ethnic myths, music
& mannerisms; an agglomeration, a
mélange (hoarded from across the seas like vulgar
secrets), some of the sum of particulars from
the hierarchy of their lowly folks' folk
inheritances: (Ha Ha) polkas & jigs &
flings & reels; & airs & tunes
& strains & chants & shouts.
                    Distilled extrinsic
vestiges (Doodah) that drip, drop, dribble, spew & spout:
a hybrid olio sluice, siphoned through the A-
MERICAN negro, without, the alarmed elite fear,
"our sanction or supervision & will culminate
in a crescendoing slosh & swirl, reshaped
in the vessel of its newfound mold: A-
MERICAN MINSTRELSY in BLACK FACE,
Black Face *"a person made up as a Negro . . .*
make-up used by performers of Negro roles,
usually exaggerated
                    for comic effect," Doodah Doodah Da.

Still,
at first & for a time they theater
together: the new made in A-MERICA
working class "just folks" folks in their "pit"
& whores & aspiring sow's-ear rag-ruffians,
immigrants & blacks, each in their separated
sections, segregated from the similarly
segregated silk-purse whites in their boxes,

for a programme as varied as the mix & flux
of its onlookers:
                    songs & dances comic &
somber, arias, recitatives witty or
bleak, *comedia dell'arte*: mocking but mild

ridicules & broader burlesques on the conduct
& crudities of said foreigners, rustics, coloreds
& fools.

It's 'round about then (late 1830s),
when Abolitionists are demonized as Damn
Yankee interlopers; a fractious array of
free blacks, Quaker quacks, meddling moralist
dogmatics, free soil fanatics, Union partisans,
radical Republicans, all with their absurdist,
cutting wedge notions of the (Hah Hah) humanity
of niggers.

Figures.

"It's the redman's fault in the first damn place," many think.
"If they'd displayed any aptitude for work or
authority the Africans could have been
left where they were."

"We're better off here," we slaves are told, "than back
in our African land of old. So much better off
we should be overjoyed, here, in A-MERICA,
at least we're employed. & since we're 'naturally' fit
for labor 'too low for whites' our presence means
the good old U.S.A. benefits too, by our lack
of rights." Well, alright.

Aside: 1835 Sierra Leon: Sengbe Pieh (c. 1813–1879), father of
3, is kidnapped by 4 men on a narrow road. He is coffled & passes,
in the cadence of currency, from hand to hand, ending in the clutches
of Spaniard slavers. Is shipped, packed shoulder to shoulder, to
Havana. In an additional act of dupery his captors diddle or *dudeldopp*
the law banishing the import of African slaves into Cuba. Pieh's
African origins are masked. On the manifest he is shackled with a
non-African alias. More later . . .

& In 1836 P. T. Barnum sings *"Zip Coon"* & other *"Ethiopian" songs* in
Camden, South Carolina. He does it in Black Face. Doodah.

&

in 1838,

FREDERICK BAILEY:

(c. 1817–1895)

(Speaks)

I was afflicted with an incurable case of *Drapetomania*, even before it was *"discovered"* in the 1850s by Samuel A. Cartwright, surgeon & psychologist, practicing in Louisiana, a.k.a. the Pelican, the Bayou, the Creole, the Mardi Gras, the Cajun State. Louisiana purchased by Thomas Jefferson in 1803 after the slave uprising led by a black general.

TOUSSAINT-LOUVERTURE:

(1743?–1803)

(Speaks)

We dispatched 24,000 of Napoleon's armies' finest occupiers from our land.

Napoleon Bonaparte (1769–1821), French general, emperor, who'd previously bragged to being the successor, not of Louis XVI (1754–1793), but of Charlemagne (742?–814), a.k.a. Charles the Great, son of Pepin the Short. After Rome fell to its knees, Charlemagne (with the nod from the pope) invaded Italy & Moorish Spain, hence he became the emperor of the West.

Bonaparte said, *"I love power. But it is as an artist that I love it. I love it as a musician loves his violin, to draw out its sounds and chords and harmonies."* Said, *"There are two levers for moving men — interest and fear."*

Then had to reconsider all that big talk when his own men were routed by my Haitian rebels. & in fear for their lives moved swiftly out of Haiti. *"Damn sugar, damn coffee, damn colonies!"* Bonaparte declared, revising the tune to which he'd set all that big time emperor-speak.

FREDERICK BAILEY:

Cutting his losses Napoleon unloaded Louisiana & split the Americas
like a runaway slave booking for the border after coming down with
the dreaded *Drapetomania. Drapetomania* was the freedom disease,
a notion Cartwright'd come up with to explain what a runaway'd
come down with to cause a runaway's running away. The freedom
disease. *Drapetomania.* Said to fuse the Greek for *"runaway slave"* with
"crazy." Even the O.E.D. didn't buy it, neither does Google. But Dr.
Cartwright, in the finest scientific tradition, used it to portray the
mental disease that *"induces the negro to run away from service, [and] is as
much a disease of the mind as any other species of mental alienation, and much
more curable, as a general rule."*
Doctor Cartwright's prescription for cure was, when the wretches
were recaptured, to whip *"the devil out of them."*
I *"steals" my* self from "service." In my mind I radically reckons
I have as much right to my self & the goods &
services produced thereof as the man & the
system that holds the papers on my person. &
in a reasoned proclamation of self emancipation
slips the hostile bonds of servitude & shucks my
slave appellation. Appropriating a new
surname from an outlaw in Sir Walter Scott's novel
The Lady of the Lake, I double the final
S, ending my new identifying proper
noun with the look of cakewalking serpents. Frederick
Douglass, is born. I will, like Scott's Douglas, as do
all fugitive kind, practice to deceive as I
negotiate the tangled web of a world of
minstrels, peppered with barbarous clans burning crosses
on hilltops. Doodah, indeed. My name is not all
I, the former Bailey, will change.

1839

SENGBE PIEH:

I, Sierra Leonian, Joseph Cinque, a.k.a. Cinques, a.k.a. Cinquez,
a.k.a. Jinques, a.k.a. Jingua, a.k.a. Sinko, née Sengbe Pieh, was
kidnapped & enslaved to Cuba & there resold. Bound by buckras for

Puerto Principe, I with 50 or so other captives *"ironed hand and foot"*
& chained in a line, waist to neck aboard *"the black schooner"* Amistad,
Spanish for "Friendship," Doodah. It is long, low & black with a
narrow white stripe. It has decks of mahogany. In its hold we share
space with a cargo of gold doubloons. The tide turns when the human
cargo rises up. The Captain, the cook & 2 others of the slave brig's
crew are killed. We spare 5, order them to navigate to Africa. The
survivors bamboozle us by setting a circuitous course to nowhere.
We, the *"Amistads"* are arrested when we drift into American waters.

The foppish 5′6″ *"Little Magician,"* a.k.a. *"Martin Van Ruin,"* a.k.a.
Martin van Buren (1782–1862), is former vice-president under
Andrew Jackson, a.k.a. *"one of the people,"* is eighth President of the
United States & the 1st not born a British subject or of British blood.
Van Buren, a.k.a. *"The Red Fox of Kinderhook."*

EYE OF THE BLACK VOICE:
(Also see John Elroy Sanford, a.k.a. Redd Foxx [1921–1991]),
to appease his Southern pro-slavery support says, in essence,
"Fugg It!!" to Pieh & his boys.
Van Buren insists the Amistads be tried for piracy & murder.
One hundred 39 years too late for Van Buren or the prisoner,
Abigail Van Buren, a.k.a. "Dear Abby," a.k.a. Pauline Friedman
Lederer, advises,
"The best index to a person's character is (a) how he treats people who can't do
him any good, and (b) how he treats people who can't fight back."

SENGBE PIEH:
The press of 1839 wonders & the
courts deliberate: are Pieh & the Amistads
assassins or mutineers, possessions or
privateers? Cannibals, Cubans, cargo, savages,
slaves or kidnappees, or debauchees? Is it a
property issue cut & dried, for a provincial
court to decide? or a national calamity
subject to the Chief Executive's rumination?
or perhaps the royal arbitration of Her

Britannic Majesty? Questions of whether 'tis
matters of teatime opinion or legality,
a *cause célèbre*, or not? careen off each other
like marbles in a shaken chamber pot.

Cross cut: abolitionists scold & sermonize.

While entertainers act: &/so, within days, a minstrel show melodrama,

> The Black Schooner
> —or the—
> Pirate Slaver Amistad!

is launched at a Bowery Theatre,
corner of Broadway and Ann Street,
across the from City Hall.

> *"A new Nautical Drama founded on the late extraordinary*
> *Piracy! Mutiny! & Murder!"*

SENGBE PIEH:

The *"Amistads"* & the crew survivors, hired
or inspired by their captors or benefactors
act as if we are actors, appear on stage in
cameo roles. &, so, again, it is not our
true selves: e.g., sons, orphans, subjects, craftsmen,
fathers, brothers, planters, husbands, criminals, hunters,
that our stage presence represents, our present condition,
player pawns: captives in America that the
public pays to see.

We, & THE BLACK SCHOONER are but part of an evening's fare
of Barnum-like amusements, with

LE PETITE ANDREAS,
the Infant Phenomenon,
&
an Asiatic Historical Drama,
&
Fire Worshipper,
&
Grand March & Procession

by, among others, a band of Black Eunucks,
accompanied by the silver bells of the Muezzin
& a Christian trumpet,
on their return from their Pilgrimage from Mecca,
dressed in white,
with bracelets and collars of gold.

In the programme I am billed as Zemba Cinques, an African, Chief of
the Mutineers.
Receiving 6th billing is *"Cudjo, a deformed Dumb Negro."* The Amistads,
are credited collectively as *"Slaves &c,"* are functional but otherwise
nameless (as are the Black Eunucks). That is enough for the public.
The play is the thing. The play is a hit!

In our first depictions in public print the *"Amistads"* (not by our given
names that they are known, but by phonetic epithets, that fit the A-
MERICAN tongue & ear: Apolonio, Andrew, Antonio, Augustine,
Bartholomew, Bartolo, Caledonis, Casmiro, Celistino, Corsino,
Desiderio, Dionecio, Edward, Epifanio, Escalastico, Estanilaus,
Evaristo, Ezidiquiel, Francis, Frederick, Gabriel, Genancio, Hipiloto,
Hippoloto 2d, Julian, Julius, Lacis, Larduslado, Leon, Lewis,
Manuel, Martin, Mercho, Nicholas, Paschal, Phillip, Raymond,
Santario, Saturnio, Simon Peter, Stephen, Tevacio, Thomas,
Tidoro, Venito, Vicinto, & Zidnon &, perhaps, depending on your
source, Bowle, Fuliwa, Grabaung, Gootah & Jooeh & Kimbo,
purchased for $450 per among them) are reduced, along with any
notion of our names, or ways, to camera obscura silhouettes, wraith
images perceived through a small opening & traced to defaced,

Physiognomical profiles. They are faceless blackened faced blacks,
cipher celebrities, they are disembodied shadow-show still lifes.
Multiples of 1.
&/so
it is,
as it so often will be, when being presented to the curious public-eye
for its collective inspection & edification, *"they"* (purchased at $450
per) remain *"they,"* each a *tabula rasa*, a shady caricature. Featureless.
An enigma without content, as dark & impenetrable, it is thought, if
considered at all, as the continent of their origin. Multiples of 1.
I am made the gnomon,
the object that light shines on
causing a projected shadow that darkens all behind it.
"And the lamplight o'er him streaming throws his shadow on the
floor;"
Edgar Allan Poe writes 15 years hence,
"And my soul from out that shadow that lies floating on the floor,
Shall be lifted—nevermore!"
A white newspaper says of me, there was nothing
"to *mask him* as a malicious man," says,
on the block I would fetch a good $1,500.
Another white paper reports my
"cleanliness would compare advantageously
with any colored dandy on Broadway. He was calm and collected."
The Colored American says I am "a royal fellow,"
says I have the look
"not so much of the warrior as the sage,"
says shameless whites "have made merchandise of the likeness
of Cinques."
Another white paper reports me to be
"a dumpish looking negro . . .
[one of] the vilest animals in existence,
perfectly contented in confinement,
without a ray of intelligence, and sensible only
to the wants of the brute." The eye
of the beholder & all that
Doodah. Evermore.

P. T. BARNUM:

It's only a couple years hence,
1841,
      the year the Supreme Court
upholds the *Amistad* Africans' freedom &
the Anti-Slavery Society of Massachusetts
hires Frederick Douglass to fill a full-time
lecturer line, that Scottish eye doctor James Baird
(1796–1860) first fiddles
      with *hypnosis*,
noun, A state usually induced by another
in which the subject may experience heightened suggestibility.
Coined after the Greek word *sleep*, which rimes with *sheep.*
Synonyms: insensibility, obtuse-ness . . .
& I, P. T. Barnum, later of
      "The Greatest Show on Earth,"
tinkers, cobbles. Think good old American
ingenuity, inventiveness. Spunk: Think
Edison, Ford, Carver. See me open my
American Museum,
   . . . mental imperceptiveness, stupor, coma, trance . . .
                 a Mecca of
oddities & enticements.
               . . . senselessness, impassivity . . .

THE PEERLESS PRODIGIES OF PHYSICAL PHENOMENA
AND GREATEST PRESENTATION OF MARVELOUS LIVING HUMAN CURIOSITIES

I, like hypnosis,
like anesthesia, like Lamont Cranston
(1930–1954), a.k.a.
The Shadow, a.k.a. Kent Allard, masked man (nudge
nudge) had the power to *cloud men's minds* by numbing,
or dumbing their (collective) consciousness, just like
ol' Jung's, Swiss shrink Carl (1875–
1961), shadow self:
    . . . unconsciousness, unintelligence . . .
the dark matter
of the self's disowned.
. . . & moral insensibility . . .

          The Shadow, like me, knew
what evil lurks in the hearts of men. Yet, when common
wisdom buzzed my ear, I, P.T., disagreeing,
employed my common dollar & cents sense,
foreseeing profitable potential in giving
heed to the greed & needs of the new-created
sludge progeny mass class, *"common, unkempt, rowdy
& loud,"* materializing from the viscera
of Industrialization. I foresaw them in spare-
time pursuit of distractions to escape the cramp
& grime of their tenement sties, with (after rent,
bread, butter, buckles & ribbons) burning itches
of surplus wages in their britches, *"Every crowd
has a silver lining."* Thus I spake, though did
not say *"There's a sucker born every minute,"* though
will, knowing a good line when I hear one, not
disclaim it. & opens, in part with funds
        (FOLLOW THE MONEY!)
from my Joice Heth ruse, my hall of hoaxes,

my American Museum, finding, finally
in the over spilling glut, the Formula; the
balance of base & sublime: an alter-world
of seductions, acquired, conserved & put on
show, for the amusement, uplifting moral
instruction, citizenship tutoring &
satisfaction of the heterogeneous
appetites of the emerging menagerie
of the new publics. That uneasy armistice
between genteel Top Downs & earthy Bottom Ups
eyeing each other across borders & boundaries
with wary airs—as they stepped right up, forked over
The Single Low Fee for Admission, 25 cents,
kids a dime, then toddled right in, into, in the
Greek sense of it, a shrine to the Muses &
marveled at the flux:

SPECTACULAR!! EDUCATIONAL!! FREAKS! FREAKS! FREAKS!

Broadway corner of Printers Row, New York, N.Y.
. . . *narcotism, narcosis & twilight sleep*
. . . which rimes with *sheep*.

My hall features, to my millions of enticee's
delight, *"The Happy Family,"* in the same cage
1 panther, 1 lion, 1 tiger + 1 white
fleeced little lamb. "The display will become a
permanent feature," says I, "if the supply
of lambs holds out."
                                    B'dumpt dum!
Curiosities advertised as half a million.
History, art & science. All & all a
superfluity of novelties; plethora
of fascinations; blustering fete of come-ons;
eccentricities, clap-trap & treasures. A

congress of the greatest vegetable, mineral,
animal & human anomalies. A
profusion, an extravagance, ostentation
of *"exotic new species"*; a satiety
of the different from the normal; the rarely seen;
deviations from the accepted — (as the new
mass knew themselves thought to be
— in the tongue of the times — *nature's mistake)* — freaks,
at best once removed from my array of full freaks;
the worst. A Noah's Ark of God's cursed. Oddities,
amassed at grave peril, great expense & mortal
danger to man, critters & creatures — furry, feathered,
scaled, 2 legged & 4 alike; *"discovered"* in far-
flung corners & climes; varied-colored alien
natives & their (un)natural *au naturel*
animal propensities, presented through my
benevolence for one fourth of a dollar in
dioramic *papier-mâché delineations*
of their native habitants, for their intimate,
uninhibited, uninterrupted, startling
& wondrous & fearsome & joyous "But for
the grace of God" . . . inspection & edification.

See, as prime proof, 2 or 3 examples,
depending on how I tallied the conjoined
Chang & Eng. Twins. Siamese. Who, if you do or
don't please, when they retire from my employ enjoy
a 60 grand nest egg; do as they desire:
take as their bride 2 Tar Heel maidens, abide in
houses divided, sire 22 offspring &
become that worrisome thing, 2 faced knaves: owners
of slaves.

& the 2nd, or 3rd, or
                                 &

General Tom Thumb
née, Charles S. Stratton
(1838–1883)

MAN IN MINIATURE
SMALLEST MAN ALIVE!
40 INCHES AT HIS HEIGHT

For me, they say, No Low Too Low in
my Museum, How'd I calculate the
little General, do you reckon? they snicker.
As 1, or half, or perhaps three-fifths a man?
The latter, as less than full was how the author
of *"all men are created equal,"* America's
3rd President, Tom Jefferson gauged the enslaved?
If measured by box office income little Tom
was worth his weight & then some, as were Uncle Tom's
3/5ths, in gold.
      All in all a brazen & bizarre
bazaar, astounding & plain packed
packaged in the 5 storied mish mash hocus pocus
magnum opus of truth & sham: significant
& trivial: an almanac of specimens,
relics & memorabilia: the rich reaping
of a random harvest, displayed in niches, halls,
crannies, on shelves, on tables, on walls, hooks & in
jugs, jars, nooks, pots, boxes, bottles, vials, books &
aquaria, in aisles, on easels & on stages,
under glass, in compartments, cubbyholes, in cabinets
& in cages. Statutes & automatons: canvas,
wax, wood, plaster, human & stone: freestanding,
hanging, in groups & alone. Images: stenciled,

etched, sketched, rubbed, imprinted &
engraved: portraiture, architectural &
pastoral; photographs, ferrotypes, handbills, cartoons,
transparencies, broadsides, caustic, in memory,
satirical; of people, places & events,
renowned or inglorious, but preferably,
for my part & my patrons, demanding,
infamous &/or notorious. & lectures
& sermons, sanctimonious, without shame or
apology, on patriotism &
family life's vices: dumb shows, *tableaux vivants*; &
"The American Moral Drama: Uncle Tom's Cabin"
& Shakespeare: slideshows & the latest ridiculous
& ingenious devices 19th century
industrial vision & capital could produce.
& all proper: family fare:

No Chewing or Spitting,
no characters of appalling repute,
No Intoxicating Liquors or Low Language,
& of course, those of African descent
NOT ALLOWED.

&
It is beyond dispute
THE MOST MARVELOUS CREATURE LIVING

PADDY:
(Erin's son, ould sod's exile, a minstrel "delineator")
It is "Zip the Pinhead," the "What-Is-It?" the
African missing link, half human half orang-

outang is what Barnum would have our swarm believe.
To our delight it rattled its cage & jabbered
gibberish, then saw'd at a fiddle & jigged.

Managed by (nudge nudge) Captain O. K. White.
What it was, was William Henry Johnson (18-
42/3–1926) you guessed it, a black man.

Yes, Mister Phineas Taylor Barnum, master,
Prince of the All American Humbug. To let
him catch us off balance was bait on his hook; to
be reeled in by some bamboozle we (later)
allowed had sounded too good to be true, but
credulity of need had got the better of
our best judgment — nudge nudge — like our following the

TO THE EGRESS

sign, & at the closed door, we stood, like wave upon
numberless, nameless waves of tillers & toters,
tiptoed at the rail of likely former slave ships,
peering through dawn's fog for first glimpse of New York's
storied shore; keen now for the rare spectacle, by
this unknown name, "Egress" Barnum, in his
extravagance had in store — hippopotami?
beluga whales? some exotic parti-feathered
fowl? or fancied up kickshaw or gewgaw. We entered
to find ourselves exited; locked out in the Ann Street
alley behind the Museum. We stood with the
dawning we'd been duped, & it'd take a new 2 bits
offer to P.T.'s coffer
                    (for the rich a mere
pittance for their re-admittance),
              but for us, the 1's
of many, a lesson: an American
experience worth twice the price! Ha ha.
We, however impolitic or ill-bred, had

put our money on the barrelhead & taken
a quarter of a dollar gamble, same as any
of the Select Few were advantaged to do, &
in the bargain shared an opportunity to
be equally hood-winked by the crafty creator
of this Happy Family of American
spectator-consumers. It let us re-see our selves —
no-land's men with dirt behind our ears, knobs on our
tongues — through these singular creatures, as, if not
feline in the fullness of its ferocity,
a leap, at least from being lamb, ewe or ram. Well,
Hell, we accept that, we do, as a bargain fair
& true.

BARNUM:
Yes, chortling, I agree, as I stacked my quarters,
& thus it would be, long (nudge nudge) as the supply
of lambs hold out.
Was years before they said it that I'd heard the
incoming scorned, the Paddys, Tonys, Shmuels &
Hans' among them:

MICK:
(Aspirant immigrant have not)
We seek an amusement, a public entertainment
that is US, that suits our lunch pail, new city concerns
& urban urges: the push & prod; the smut &
guts; the rude & crude hustle & bustle & clang
& bang & bellow, brawl & brawn. & an amusement
of anvil sparks, chop, scoop, blast, choo choo, Whoop-Pee! &
TIM-BER! of the Wild Frontier of our Manifest
Destiny. A public entertainment for our
here & our now, that defines, defends & excuses
US; embodies & emboldens & warrants US;
nurtures our notions of adaptation & adoption.
An amusement that vindicates, uplifts &
enables our aspirant A-MERICAN notions;

allows US to pine for a past that was never present
& believe only what we see & yet not re-
late, relive (re-)turn to our recently ceded
hearth & shore, our realm of yore, our other, our
Mother Land,

          2 *THREE*, 4.

                  A common-
denominator consumer diversion, that
in its democracy, in these heady days of
Territorial Expansion, Gold Rush, Mexican-
American War, post Haitian, French & American
Revolutions, ethnic ablutions & the
abolition of slavery in France, points US, at
the possibility of escapist stepping
stones to scale the bulwark of Refinement &
Gentility & clamber to the plateau of
that mark-making, cake-taking trip aboard the
gravy-train of Equality to The Promised Land
of high-hog living,

          2, *THREE*, 4.

In his garden of grotesques Barnum gave refuge
& value added, wooing & leaving us wide eyed
& wowed, as if bewitched. He'd found, in due course,
what separated us from our excess & drew us
in, time & again, weary, from the storm of scorn
we weathered day by day. It was not simply
the Spectacle, this weird Wonder or that,
that sated us as we grazed lazily in his vineyard
of forbidden fruit. What he offered,

                  Let

the buyer beware,

          that we needed, like work or air,
was the what we wanted of what we wanted:
the Consumer's Choice, fair & square; privilege to
pick & pluck from among the many; be observers,
not the watched; civilized; judge; jury. Here,
for a quarter of a dollar, a nickel &

2 thin dimes, in Barnum's orchard of otherness,
we're stationed at the scale by the bell of the horn
of plenty, free to chose.
                          The envied inverse
of the mete & dole—deemed our due—of husks & rinds
contested for with dogs, niggers & rats on the
metropolis' horse dunged cobblestones. Herein,
we, according, solely, to our taste & whim,
select from the harvest of fruit of our new knowledge
of our rethought selves; which to buy (let mesmerize)
which to let lay by. The choices, no more, no less,
than available to any gentleman or
citizen, say.

MISTER E. S. WELBOURNE:
(refined: defies, denies & defines. Bemoaning)
Oh woe this restless hoard with their outlandish tastes
tuned to mulligan stew, ragout, goulash & borscht,
with breeding & bearing to match. They quiver like
youngsters on the eve of Christmas. Their patience with &
tolerance for other forms fade as they hoot &
clomp, bleat & blather at the edifying &
polished portions of the programme's quality fare,
& each night, voice their choice for entertainment base
& trite. Black Face parodists pop up like topsy,
sprouting, like invidious weeds, between the
lilies of the evening's acts. Much to their callow
unread & ribald delight, Black Face skits sop their
loutish appetite.

PADDY & MICK:
(Enthused)
We are sanctified & consecrated in the
spirit of A-MERICA by our anointing
from the fountains of Barnum & Black Face. It is
step *ONE*, 2, *THREE*, forward toward claiming an
A-MERICAN self & wielding united influence

with our lettered betters.

MISTER E. S. WELBOURNE:
(Piqued)
The being & reek of Black Face,
"a person made up as a Negro . . .
make-up used by performers of Negro roles,
usually exaggerated for comic effect,"
filled with this confounded compounding of the
slog-toiler's pooled interactions, tastes & sweats, is
a venomous blend in a befouled pool, gorged with the
grit & silt of lumpen folklore. It is offensive
to our well-bred security & senses. &
the insurgent immigrants & other ignorant
personage's rabid passion for Black Face acts,
is simple & conclusive proof of their lack
of capacity to rise above the level
of the darkies so precisely portrayed beyond
the footlights of their boundless euphoria.

VOICE OF THE BLACK EYE:
& thus it is that with the coming notion of Black Face
"a person made up as a Negro . . .
make-up used by performers of Negro roles, usually exaggerated for comic
effect"
&, Doodah, comes the notion — Welbourne's dreaded
(self fulfilling?) nightmare —
of the crack & crash of cultures,
ratatattat. The notion, ratatattat, of
the under-classes, those dark, those swarthy, those
olive-hued, those aspirants to A-MERICAN

FREE WHITE PERSONAGE (Ha Ha) ratatat &
the over-classes, the descendants of so-called
distinction, the afore-mentioned, ordained FREE WHITE
PERSONS, the High & the low clash over their
contrary notions of legitimate (nudge nudge)
entertainment.

PADDY:

Threatens, like the Mississippi in the spring time,
to glut the streams, rills & rivulets of Classicism,
Culture & Good Taste & wash away the sea wall
of the Well-Off's self-claimed & so-called Cultural
& Moral authority, despoiling the so-
called sanctity, the very foundation of
their so-called sanctuary of Privilege &
Entitlement.
(Concluding, in the daunting & confounding
spirit & philosophy of the approaching
post-Jacksonian times.)
*"If a little is good, more than enough should be
just right."*

WELBOURNE:

A threat! This egregious example of the up-
starts influence!

VOICE OF THE BLACK EYE:

influence. n. 1. an influx.
*2. originally, the supposed flowing of an ethereal
fluid or power from the stars, thought to affect the
characters and actions of people.*
*3. (a) the power of a person or group to produce effects without the exertion
of physical force of authority, based on wealth, social position, ability, etc. . . .
in'flu.ence. v. . . . to exercise or have influence on; to modify or affect in some
way; to act on; to bias; to sway . . ."*

WELBOURNE:

Influence, welded by the ballots cast at the
box office by these graceless blackened faced wastrels;
the pall of 1 man 1 vote popularism
(where the results are valued far beyond their worth).
A threat! A threat! A threat! Not only in the
theater arena, but, by extension,
a threat to scuttle the Holy bonds of Family,
Citizenship, Politics & State.

VOICE OF THE BLACK EYE:

Neither Welbourne nor Paddy notes, nor admits, *ratatattat*, nor
comments on the commonality of their basic (or base) desire: having
someone to lord over & laugh at. Doodah, Doodah, Doodah Doodah
Da. UMPH! UMPH!

WELBOURNE:

(Frets)
It is due to this unsettling surge in the
unwashed's census that we, the better sorts, sense is
of the rise of a fending, perhaps unbending
prevailing wind. A threat, strong enough to stir
the standards atop the staffs staking out the
parameters of our Cultural encampment.
A change threatening change. Unchecked change. Change beneficial
to, or set in motion by the likes of "a
motley rabble of saucy boys, negroes &
mulattos, Irish teagues & outlandish jack tarrs,"
is change uncontrolled, unreasoned & un-
reasonable. Without plan or master. Blind.
Threatening doom to the sanctity of their sapsweet
harmony with Nature's manifest forward march
2, *THREE*, 4.
                    An order creeping along at its
languorous pace since yesterday & yesterday
& yesterday. Set to a comfortable, steady,
legitimate, innocent cadence: sow, harvest,

market, equinox to equinox. In place, as
God intended, since the evening & the morning
after darkness (nudge nudge) *was* upon the face
of the deep,

>2, *THREE*, 4.

VOICE OF THE BLACK EYE:

change (chanj) *v.* 1.a. to cause to be different. b. To give a completely
different form or appearance to; transform . . . 3. to exchange or
replace with another . . . 4.a. to lay aside, abandon, or leave for
another, switch.

WELBOURNE:

But, in answer, early on, to our prayer, according to
our notions of it, & further proof of our being
"God's chosen," according to our notions of that,
we see few signs 'mongst the rabble rank and foul, white
& black, of the taking of or making of off-
stage strides t'ward crossing one another's lines: color
or social or political or economic
or educational, of our, or their notions
of those.

SENGBE PIEH:

&/so, 1841, the year arc lamps are tried in Paris,
we, the *"Amistads,"* are tried before the United States Supreme Court.
It begins on February 22, George Washington's birthday.
Despite a death threat to our defense counselor,
promising to *"stop the music,"*
our *"old man eloquent,"*
the 74 year old former President of the U.S., John Quincy Adams

(1767–1848), played on.

During the 2 years of our incarceration 2 of *"the captives,"* the Mende speaking *"Amistads,"* have died of *"white flux."* Diarrhea. We survivors have been instructed in English & Theology.

After Adam's 4½ hour opening day opening statement a slave, unnamed, finds one of the Justices dead in the night. Adams' continued reasoning eloquence convinces the remaining 8 that the *"Amistads"* were guiltless as charged of having *"absolved"* ourselves. We are freed.

But, still, freed we (Apolonio, Andrew, Antonio, Augustine, Bartholomew, Bartolo, Caledonis, Casmiro, Celistino, Corsino, Desiderio, Dionecio, Edward, Epifanio, Escalastico, Estanilaus, Evaristo, Ezidiquiel, Francis, Frederick, Gabriel, Genancio, Hipiloto, Hippoloto 2d, Julian, Julius, Lacis, Larduslado, Leon, Lewis, Manuel, Martin, Mercho, Nicholas, Paschal, Phillip, Raymond, Santario, Saturnio, Simon Peter, Stephen, Tevacio, Thomas, Tidoro, Venito, Vicinto & Zidnon &, perhaps, depending on your source, Bowle, Fuliwa, Grabaung, Gootah & Jooeh & Kimbo, purchased for $450 per among them) still remain "they," "them," "the Amistad negroes," "Mendians," a problem presence. Lumped. *Them.* As if we were a single, 1 size fits all entity, as with Minstrel's representations, as if 1 was no different than another. Multiples of 1. As if our pre-enslavement status, point of origin, language, situations did not matter. Blackened out faceless black faces captured & marketed by the phrase, Black wretches.

Stranded still.

VOICE OF THE BLACK EYE:
& also in 1841 *"Deutschland, Deutschland über Alles"* is published in
Germany,
& the first ad agency is formed, & after 7 months a wagon train of
emigrants,
led by an Irish-American, reaches California.
& New Zealand becomes Britain's latest colony,
& New York houses 300,000, Ireland tops 10 million,
7 mill less than the U.S.,

& those strewn mostly in towns of 2,000 or so. 1841, Irish farms fall in decay, potatoes are the staple, whiskey is cheaper than bread, black slavery has been outlawed since 1171, & Daniel O'Connell, speaking from Ireland, calls, in his multi-thousanded voice, for their Irish-in-A-MERICA brethren to be for LIBERTY FOR ALL, to CLING BY THE ABOLITIONISTS. O'Connell's nickname the Liberator. Later, oh, woe, under pressure from papal princes & Southern persons of property (soil & souls) O'Connell, the Liberator, capitulates, recants, rebukes Garrison & his anti-black slavery writings in (nudge nudge) The LIBERATOR, 2, *THREE*, 4.

RALPH WALDO EMERSON:
(U.S. intellectual [1803–1882])
"Trust men, and they will be true to you; treat them greatly, and they will show themselves great."

PADDY:
The point, according to my notion of it,
America is not a gold-paved path for the
frayed, or foreign, or fettered foot. Not Eden with
apples of His eye, pleading for the picking. Come
to that, niggers, dogs & Irish bogs need not apply.
Spat on, shat on by every blooming boss &
bloody bloke, ev'ry Wave Ruler there, where we could
only consume, by their leave, potatoes we grew.
Other staples, raised by our hand, were reaped &
sent by force of bayonet & bullet to fill
English guts. & now here, the White Man & the mis-

led Abolitionists zealots! Jesus H. Christ!
Forgive me Father, forgive me for my immodest
inverse notion. I come by it honest as calf
to tit. Was Ireland's own contrarian
Jon Swift once damned the isle as vile, then turned face &
embraced her like a nubile concubine. & was
Swift, who wove stories to malign human folly,
in another about face, rove from liberal Whigs
to stable mate with straight, Old Line Tories.
But still, our current duplicitous state is no
greater than the root contradiction of A
-merica herself; that Justice should be shown as
blind with her scales balanced, is bilge. In America
it's not only that our wee ones are a meal for
the genteel, we're no better than the privies
into which they're shat. & our curse, forgive us Father,
is to be cursed for being who we cursed before
we came: shamers of the common, the down &
out-at-the-elbowed, in order to be blessed by
being thought better, at least, than the blacks. Yes, bless
us . . . , Father, we bare our contradictions, but are
of but one mind, & it is constant & rides the wings
of our will.

RASTUS:
(Free Black)
Fleeing the Fiends of our shared despair, the failed
Janus-faced sons of Blarney & Cork seek concealment
behind the false face of our sham gaiety. These
Judases, foul players with our swiped swag are but
blustering, brogue'd tongued jackdaws in the peacock
feathers of our rags. They think us naïve enough to
believe they believe it merely a masquerade,
a comrade's shared charade. As if, at some meeting
we'd missed (having not been invited) it'd been agreed
the two timers'd take the lead, be spokesmen,
progenitors of the raucously sly, stridently

wry insider's joke on the absurdity of
our mutual marginality.

PADDY:
(Applying burnt cork)
Who's so pure as to be told of a well worn trail
out of Hell & not try it because it's littered
with carrion of self interest?

RASTUS:
They, famine's famished, act like they've suffered so till
loyalty's but a lemon to squeeze for its bitter juice.

PADDY:
Nature & this Nation, when dwelling on daily
bread or being, shove sentiment into the ditch
or worse. Wolves feed on sheep. It is Nature's decree.
& the history of America is of
confiscation in the name of all good men being
free. (Not the reverse.)

RASTUS:
Act like any act is justified that delivers
them from their entanglement in the land that has
shut them out, exiled them to the great & infernal
wilderness of days & nights of dark matter &
icy pain, & thus has condensed their conscience to
cold gray rain.

PADDY:
& if we, deemed the least of Creation's links, are
to survive this universe with reason aflop
& taste the forbidden contentment of the A-
merican Good Life, we must do what we must. Lop
off our quibblings. Adjust. Persist. Enlist
necessity. It is our first, maybe our
only chance at an other than arse end result.

It is an opportunity devoutly not to be missed.

RASTUS:
Better, they think, to make an atonement with our
oppressors than to dwell with us. & though our
differences, in the eyes of the autocrats,
remain the same, they excuse their actions as
manifest expedience, adaptation,
acquiescence to the statutes & compunctions
of necessity. We name it Hypocrisy.

PADDY:
(Adding the last of his make-up)
Forgive us Father, blacks say we have sinned . . . but
the point is to be like them, but not to be them,
for to be them is to remain who we already
are: mean, base, menial. & the point of A-
merica, according to our notion of it,
is to change: to not be middling, plebeian, but
to rise up, to ascend, surmount, whether soaring,
scaling, clambering, or scrambling; to end up higher
than we began; a match with the muckety mucks,
merchants & mill owners; to have what we had not;
to be one of them for whom heads are bared. &
neither here in America, nor there, the nation
of our nativity, our longing, is a nigger,
nor paddy, nor bohunk, nor kike, nor polack, nor
frog, nor kraut, ruskie or wop inclined to be boss.
That is our notion of it.

VOICE OF THE BLACK EYE:
Ambrose Bierce, in his *Devil's Dictionary*, says: *"An immigrant is an
unenlightened person who thinks one country better than another."*
Grass greener . . . Doodah.

RASTUS:
&/so, since the sons of the lands from which they've been

scattered, gathered with us where it pleaseth us not, but
where we make our fires, knead our dough & lift our eyes,
it is with our two-faced brethren that we bow down,
as beasts, in the presence of our common foe, cursed
& maligned in our nakedness, our back sides
commonly boot-toed.
               But so desirous are
our brethren for the A-MERICA dangled
before them, that they gather conclaves of themselves
together against us, & in pursuit of the
sheaves of our crop, blacken their faces, in the notion
that due to our common exclusion & spirit
of strife they are therefore entitled to the claiming
of our ways, our spirit & our breath. & though some
capture some qualities & some quirks of our tunes
& timing their act of the so-called sayings of
Southern darkies' conundrums & crossfire quips &
slips is with-out our irony & our edge.
It is easier to make up & mock the
already made, than to be made to make up some new
thing. & it ain't critical who was the first Minstrel;
but what MINSTRELSY was meant to be, is the key,
see? what it means, & what it is, is.
                      & in their
treachery they parade their offense before their kith,
kin & our common masters. & they mock us by their
enactment, & though they gather the fruits & gleanings
of the harvest thereof, they do not make a
covenant, nor a league with us.
                  & lo, though they
know we are as far from the notion of the US
they present as their passport to the golden shore
of FREE WHITE PERSONHOOD, as they are from being
the gentry they envy, as is a mote from a
mountain, still, seek to use the blackness of our present
to whitewash the dark matter of their past.
&/so, *"Daddy Rice"* stepping forth from *"a motley*

rabble of saucy boys, negroes and mulattoes,
Irish teagues and outlandish jack tarrs," hides his face,
for he is afraid for the Taskmasters to look
on it. & his kind calls his name Jim Crow. & he
knows the burdens of his brethren in the face
of the Pharaohs of Industry, & like Moses,
prototype of his type, too, Rice, "In his
Fashionable Lyric Style," i.e., his gut-busting
nigger-speak, mocks a sundry of subjects from tea-
totaling to tall tales, to lank, ape-like Abe Lincoln
& his D.C. doings, &, like iron to lodestone,
lint to blue serge, dust to bric-a-brac, attracts
a lower-most following & seeks to lift their
minds & their spirits out of the wilderness of
the pit & deliver the B'howery B-hoys
& his performing disciples to the Promised
Land of Free White Personhood on the faith of Black Face.

VOICE OF THE BLACK EYE:
Black Face, "a person made up as a Negro . . .
make-up used by performers of Negro roles,
usually exaggerated for comic effect"

RASTUS:
& in the tempest & squall of our travail we can
only condemn them for their inequity, but
we cannot cut them off in their wickedness, for
they are piteous (caught in the peristaltic
passage, the suction & push suction & push
through the beast's belly toward the egress to
Free White Personhood). & in their need they cannot
love us, can only allege to be like us. &
exist on the ways & spirit & breath of us.
& long for the nurture of our humble fold,
knowing the truth about them-selves & us; knowing
their nightmare is not a parable, not a dream
divinely delivered, but the dark matter

of the burning, inconsumable twitch & gnaw
at the core of their being.
The corking complete, & in fraudulent disguises
of dazzling grins & zip they've donned to deride us
& parody the so-called ups & downs of the scrapes
& squirming, the stutters & flutters of dis's
& dat's, dem's, de's & d'o's of the ways of way
down South. The japery of their natural apery,
the Minstrels take the stage, & Black Face hurtles
toward its coming form.

                         & the Abolitionists
designate them insurgent shock troupe
educators as they wheel about & turn about
& do just so, so.

PADDY:
(the Minstrel taking the stage)
I wear this black face as a public service. By
appearing as one of the lowest sort, even
the greenhorn, the ignoramus, the unlettered
know, that by my not being what I appear to be,
that first & foremost, the point of the evening is
sport. & by their knowing it, we're free, absolved of
all blame, all shame, or illness of ease. If any
golden calves or holy cows of Taste, Grace, or caste
are naughtily nudged, gored or broken by what's shown
or spoken, it is not our care. If the High are
vexed, the middle galled, or the low feel overly
put upon by our burlesquish breaking of rules,
it's not yours truly at fault, it's simply my
flagrantly waggish blackened faced, wing bucking, corn
shucking, crooning, cooning, taboo tempting lampooning,
of the race of Ethiopian fools.

SENGBE PIEH:
& it comes to pass in 1842, 350 years after Columbus's blunder, the
Supreme Court, showing another face from the one that smiled on we

the *"Amistads"* a year ago, rules kidnapping a fugitive slave is property
reclamation rather than a crime, & though freed I & my fellows
remain *"they"* "them" *"the Amistads,"* *"Mendians"*; a problem presence
in America. Still. Stranded still. But a quandary solvable, our saviors
say, so long as we stay innocent, ignorant, humble. Malleable. Save
our souls, the plan goes, make us hymn singers. Holy. & find funds to
pack us back as converted missionaries to Christianize the un-clothed
heathens at home, to cast the light of the Lord on the dark face of
Africa's moral depravity.
Make the Amistads a troupe, the plan goes,
take our show on the road
we're already an ensemble.
We open with our story,
sing a tune or two, take questions at the close.
Contributions are our review.

Two and a half years after arriving we cast off from America aboard
the good ship *Gentlemen*. Doodah, nudge nudge & a wink of the eye.

MICK:
1842
"The New York game" (baseball), mechanical air conditioning,
ice making & ether as a general anesthesia are introduced.
& the *"Old* Colony State" Massachusetts, the "Bay State,"
says our working kids under 12 must have their hours
cut back to a max of 10 a day, & another
200,000 of my landsmen wave bye
to the old sod & join by steam or sail. &
it comes to pass, they, as we at the beginning
of our just ended journey, spanning space & the
process of time, we, the newcomers, the aspirant
immigrants, discover ourselves in this New Land
stamped down still, lacking resource, recourse, or
representation, taxed, as for generations,
with an inheritance of dearth & affliction,
&, as for generations, are again & still
outside the gates of the house of the lords & 1

brogue below the other on the downhill descent.
Lords of Industry here, rather than of the Land Lords
there, who, with hardened hearts equate our ethnic flux
with cur, count us imports of no import, classify
us uncouth, cast us below Nature's gaffe, Niger's brood.
&/so, stymied still, as for generations,
we émigrés, humiliated by the paucity, the
want, our pathetic lack of defense against the
failings from which we've fled — & to which we've fallen
since; & haunted by the railings of the stalking
specters of a legacy gainsaid; & afraid
of our past as our future's reflector we seek
a way to collect on A-MERICA's Promise to make
good the passage & set right our foot to the path
of FREE WHITE PERSONHOOD, for, in our hard-scrabble
Land of Opportunity scramble for the
barrel-bottom scraps, we, Minstrelsy's doers &
devotees know, if we know nothing else: not our
A,B,C's nor our 1,2,3's, we know; mainstream
& moneyed A-MERICAN ethos, acts & aims
tells us so, &/so we know, without condition
or quaver the crux & cause of our disfavor:
it
is
ourselves
&
them: coloreds (slave or free).

OL' BLACK JOE & MICK:
We are their grudging competition & are mired
neck & neck in contention for the loathed-level
labor available to both our "lazy," "mindless"
kind.

OL' BLACK JOE:
Doodah,
& it is in 1842 it is when the entertainment scales

are inexorably
tipped. The Minstrel-only Minstrel show as
marketable commercial product is born.
Legend has it that

DAN EMMETT & THE
VIRGINIA MINSTRELS

begin as a not all that special quartet
of normally solo Black Face players, convened
for a 1 time only, between acts appearance
as a band of Ethiopians in

A NEGRO CONCERT

meant to be mostly euphonious music,
respectable family fare, without the usual
grit & vulgarities of ethnic & MINSTRELSY
performances.

PADDY:

It is the form that clicks: coloreds,
plural. A coterie, a company. A Host!
Like the Amistads. All for 1. A batch of darkies,
& their amassed crackle & scratch, matched with music!
Pure genius! Inspired pluck! Stitched together odds
& ends from the favored of other forms:

                              sappy
songs & saccharine segments; fun-for-fun's-sake scenes
with an Ethiopian slant. The jostle &
hubbub of bones, banjos, tambourines & fiddles
as a fresh, only in A-MERICA
experience: a teetering-skeetering
congregation of sables!
                    & soon thereafter,
as an example of product improvement,
as the phraseology of the emerging
sales-speak will have it, Edwin Christy & his
Christy's Minstrels fine tune Emmett's wily but
serendipitous model without mode.

OL' BLACK JOE:
Christy, ably aided by *"Oh! Susannah,"*
"My Old Kentucky Home," "Camptown Races," "Old Black Joe,"
& such as pirated & repenned by A-
Merica's 1st pro songwriter, Stephen Foster
(1826 [died in the charity ward
of Bellevue Hospital]–1864).

PADDY:
Christy, sits them all down, half circle around. &/so
none of the kinsmen with blackened face has an
excuse not to know his place (nudge nudge).

RASTUS:
&/so, the notions of MINSTRELSY & BLACK FACE
are reshaped, Doodah, in the repository
of their new found form:
    A-MERICAN BLACK FACE MINSTRELS
not *"in 1,"* not the novelty, but the show,
the whole show & nothing but the slang-wanging,
ritualized, formalized, *"an every time I*
wheel about I jump Jim Crow," patented in
1843 show.
    A crazy quilt of curtain
to curtain Black Face bobs & bits: jokes, sketches,
songs, dances & skits: depictions, assumed legit,
but really fictions: commonly imagined
rollicksome apings of the frolicsome funny
business & slapstick shapings of feckless, faceless
Ethiopians' hapless woes & bon mots.

PADDY:
Comic renditions of, Doodah, the ups & downs,
& coming 'round the mountains of negro life:
a laughable lark full of congo refrains,
conundrums, laments, abolitionist's lectures
& the like.

RASTUS:

Mark the moment. Minstrelsy made modern. The meeting
of its audience & Black Face, *"a person made up as a Negro . . .
make-up used by performers of Negro roles,
usually exaggerated for comic effect."*

PADDY:

Is, instead of the same old solo vignettes of
1 man with his wise cracks, banjo & bones, now like
A-MERICA,

RASTUS:

& the Amistads.

PADDY:

An assembly of separates.

RASTUS:

& Foster's politely called "appropriations"
of the dark matter of ethnics' original efforts,
are the nucleus, the mock-up, the mold
of A-MERICAN entertainment: modeled on
the A-MERICAN plan. Is

AN EVENING'S ENTERTAINMENT!

The perfect consumable, light weight, easily
digestible, by, of & enacted for the
especial delight of the perfect consumer,
those among the evenings flock susceptible
to this class of amusement (the feckless & faceless
class & caste concocted, of rag & bone, by Barnum),
trained to queue & guzzle & gulp bountiful
supplies of common denominator quality
helpings of what they demand.

MICK:

We, we who are, in the word-stock of FREE WHITE PERSONS,

"swarthy," "olive hued," "sallow," or *"dark,"* or any
of the other cryptic or coded synonyms
associated with Mediterranean,
or *"Blackguard"* (Black Irish laggards), or Slavs, Germans,
Catholics, or kinky headed Jews, laughing, but
offstage, out of sight of that spotlight, hoping
by hiding ourselves & armed with our common sense
of our primacy over blacks, as conveniently
imagined for us in MINSTRELSY's message through
the fidgety, slow witted BLACK FACE accounts
of our lowly counterparts, we prompt, ride the haughty
& high brow of it, out on a rail, & run
the naughty & low intent back in, then that'll
mean more bounce to the bumbling ounce! More-4-for-1
bang for the all-for-fun buck, 'mongst our ruck of nether-
most musketeers. Hosanna, hip hurrah & Cheers,
Cheers, Cheers!"

RASTUS:
—Hope to cross that line from immigrant to A-
MERICAN—as they imagine that to be—i.e.,
to *"pass"*—as they imagine that to be, & bask
in the radiant & purifying golden
torchlight, as one of the anointed & certified.

MICK:
All A-MERICAN BLACK FACE MINSTRELSY is
a common, in A-MERICA, experience
we recent foreigners can embrace; draw strength from.
Share. It's as infectious & morale lifting as
martial music, as muster, as colors 'round which
to rally. It stirs the souls of soldiers &
civilians alike UMPH! UMPH!
                              So, as a wary
ruling class monitors & frets, we newcomers with
something of our own, an A-MERICAN amusement,
begin to Embrace the Place of Promise, like

a motherless, lap snuggled child . . .

RASTUS:
But, no matter how we tried to turn our backs, o'er
the next half decade we had to face it, factions
of the public pined for Paddy plays, where B'hoy:
Mose, lowly, sod simple, no capital nor means
of production, working class Mose, & Lize, his
bumpkin beau, belittled by being their own true slaughter-
house aptitude selves. Eventually, in an
act of gross irony, Mose & Lize shame-facedly
went blackface . . .

MICK:
'Tween US & the gents of standing & prosperity
is a breech broad as the briny o'er which we sailed,
pushed by mounting waves that rolled us to this hard done by
shore, where we're nearer now by a damn sight, in their
sight, to the negro element, in attitude,
environs & consequence, than to their "noble" species,
the damned dandy-doodling Yankees with their polite
& scrubbed popinjay ways & WASP disdain, who dropped us,
plop, into the thick bubbling murk of the myth
of the A-MERICAN melting pot, to stew
in this olio (nudge nudge) of hopelessness &
humiliation where all is foul & there is
no fair, no just judgment or measure from the men
of mark.

RASTUS:
Like us, "our aspiring Gaelic 'cousins'"
are seen, when seen at all, as, at best, utile; once
broken, that is, of their Old Sod ways & tempered
to the Hup 2 Three of industrial routine;
then & only then they'll be fit as prospective
cogs, sprockets, workable parts (nudge nudge)
of the awesome concoction of A-MERICA,

then & only then will they be fit for productive
vocations, then & only then minions worth their
meat, then & only then of service,
like
us, they think.

MICK:
A damnable devil's own dilemma, being
thought bootlicking dogsbodies to bluebloods, par to
niggers, or even—the cruelest cut—thought to be
blackey's lackeys. &/but in the being &
the doing, they think, we'll spotlight for them all, all
the differences between us & them—them
the blacks & them—the mercantile monarch class &
US, by God we will.

RASTUS:
&/so in the process—in the tradition
of the patriot protesters & Founding Fathers—
the aspirant immigrant pretenders pitch their
cause & plead their case, behind a blackened face . . .
make it pay.
                    Their blackening up is the immigrants'
signifying to their clansmen & signaling
to the despised but envied Other Half that their act,
their blackened faced enactment of the quirks &
aberrations of us, the raven breed, is the
true face of inferiority. These staged antics
& shenanigans, they're saying, are the "authentic"
acts & actions of actual underlings,
inferiors, sub-ordinates & deficients.
&/so it is not us, protest the aspiring
white blackened faced performers, not us.

MICK:
We're not deserving of the repelling wrath
of scavengers at the gate, but they are, them, them,

the dark mass in A-MERICA's midst.

Not because

they are black, but because they block our path to the
market place. Yes. Block it they do & black they are.
Neither is our doing. But block it they do &
black they are.

RASTUS:
&/so, as is the all A-MERICAN way, they,
Erin's ejected, that frayed brigade of failed farmers
& evicted knuckle-tough micks, who teeter
& sway on the tether tightroped over the fault
between the cliffs of black & white, they mask their
mission (& infamy), from the common eye through
the raiment of figurative sackcloth, make-up
of soot-ash & act of blackened faced white minstrelsy,
through which they commune with the all A-MERICANS
of vested interest.

MICK:
Yes, we stand, strangers, sojourners in your land,
cut off, we understand, because of the bur
of our brogue, our brash out-landish ways (nudge nudge),
for which we are plagued & impeded, &/but till
we are seen for the whiteness of our hearts, &
what we will, if allowed, become &, if allowed,
will atone for the unbearable darkness of
our being;

&

as our initiation &
act of supplication we will enter, with be-
grimed faces, signifying our need & readiness
to be bathed, blest, smiled on, readied to rise, to
pass-over the breech, cross the line (nudge nudge) salvaged.
&, when there is room, enter, into the shelter
of Free White Personhood, delivered from where we,
immigrant performers, have lingered, in the limbo

of repudiation, from behind the mask
& through grimaced grin & gritted teeth.

RASTUS:

Lumped, the newcomers, first-generation lads of
the ould land with no land, & US. Nigh. Close by.
Compacted. Forced by our mutual debilities
to bemingle, trod common cobbles in bordering
black & tan Quarters. We, Rastus & Paddy, Sambo & Mick,
the dangerous classes, lodged in sullen hives
of hovels & shanties rife with endemic
diseases that rack & wreck our mutually
lamentable lives.

RASTUS & MICK:

We're counted counterparts; thought fowl of inferior
feather, peas of a pod; the spit of the other.

MICK:

For barbarous pastimes & spirituous grog
to oil the Irish curse, we belly bars in the same
saloons, elbow to elbow. Jowl by jaw.

RASTUS:

Share bolstering airs & steps, we slaver & splatter
the same spittoons. But seldom arm in arm as co-
workers, or cohorts. Neither confederates nor
associates. Abettors. Yes. Co-conspirators.

MICK:

Yes. Accomplices, under certain settings. Yes.
But with no binding allegiances. Not partners,
other than in crime. There is, in fact, no stronger
communion on the face of it, than barreled crabs.

RASTUS:

The common shanty Irish players applying

charred cork parallels the point of Ben Jonson's
1605 *Black Masque*: it comes to the daughters
of Niger in a vision, *"for Aethiopes*
never dreame: their difference (blackness) isn't beautiful
as they'd deemed." A bath in Britannia waters (a
female personification of England that is)
was the only way to erase their dark disgrace
& scour themselves of their symbolic curse, & bathe
to rid they did.
        P.S.:
        Queen Anne of Denmark
(1574–1619), consort
of England's James I, commissioned the black Masque
so she & her posse could blacken up & pretend
they were Moors.
        P.P.S.
        Apparently
curiosity, or was it concern, about
the matter of darkness, or was it dark matter,
was in. The bard's Othello first strutted upon
the stage 'round about that time.
All that to say the Johnny-come-lately-Irish-
hoping-to-be-A-Merican-squatters, in their
foul play, play us (nudge nudge) & make it pay, as they
stake their claim by flaunting our false face
to an audience as wondering &/but
unknowing of our true identity, as the
mystery of the kingdom of God; an audience,
craving a fraternity of aspirations,
awe & noisy amusements, that put a face (nudge
nudge) on the A-MERICAN bogey men &
fee-faw-fums. & the witnesses of the blackened faced
white MINSTRELS mimicry are assured & reassured;
seeing, they see &/but do not comprehend our
complexity; &/so the imposters impressions
are received & seized with a sense of certitude,
cheer & reality, & all the while our

imitators, with inequity in their tongue,
whisper to us that their performance is a form
of protest on our mutual behalves. &/so
speak out of both sides of their beguiling mouths with
forked tongues & fanged intent, &, as if larceny
praises the victim, they profess that imitation
is (nudge nudge & a wink of the eye) flattery
in its sincerest form.
    The double-dealer's dis-
embodying thievery does embody an
homage (albeit unconscious) signified by
their awed admiration (albeit unconscious)
for our approach & energy &/but our
forbidden & foreboding spirit &/or our
survivors soul.
   Perhaps.
     Or
perhaps it is yet another coil of entrapping
contradiction for the delineators, or worse,
backlash of irony. The blackened faced whites know
it is us they owe &, admitted or no, they
are entoiled by their debt, for, as by Victor Hugo's
reckoning of it, "A creditor is worse than a slave-owner;
for the master owns only your person, but a creditor
owns your dignity, and can command it."
We can, by our presence sap the supposed qualities
of worth, esteem, honor, rank & respect
attendant to it by their knowing, as we &
Hugo, French novelist, dramatist & poet
(1802–1885), do, of societal
injustice, human suffering & relentless
pursuit & of buckraism's attempt to conceal
its false appearance of strength.

Is, I wonder, their playing at being us,
as if it's their privilege, simply skullduggery?
sure as shooting trespass? out & out poaching?

honest to God pilferage? bona fide scrumping
& scrounging? twenty-four karat flinching? bald-faced
burglary? clear cut, self-evident daylight
robbery?

It is, in part at least, the titillation
of role reversal, the joke to joker traversal.
It is their pre Free White Person rehearsal
for their hankered after higher station. Their
trivialization, to join the Nation.

It is their chance, through their guffaws at our kinks,
fortissimo & flaws to soothe the burr in their
craws, defer the taste of crow, boot leather & shit.
That is it. & is behind it their forsaking of
their non-nurturing mother-land, where disparity
of tongue, creed, or breeding bred bullying, beating
& butchery to the woesome wrath of sneering
laughter.

It is the voyeur's voyage of the former soil-
serf's schizophrenic homesickness for an
oxymoronic Never-Never Land of the
familiar & exotic.

Is the root of the wrong the pressure to belong?
They are our spiritnapping cousins. 1 eyed
jacks from the jump; mugs half hidden in the
duplicitous shadows of their lurking purpose?
Their contriving striving borne with them from their
blighted patches back 'ome? Was their snide 2 faced
conniving born with their maiden stridings on this
Golden shore? Was the deal to sell our souls for their
assimilation struck in Erin, or in mid
ocean meditation?

Yes. That is it. We are their first step up. Their first

A-

MERICAN hurrah.

That First Freedom afforded in-comers in to
the A-MERICAN flock: a cover of darkness
behind which to bemock *&* skulk from their stinging
past. A trespassing through the racial chiaroscuro.
The hidden, forbidden consummation
through the eradication of the pale face of
impotent Otherness, via the cosmetic
& curative putting on (nudge nudge) of lamp black
or burnt cork; the enthrallment of the obscuring
gradation into the foreboding (dare I say)
heart of darkness, o'er the threshold of an opening
then closing door.

MICK:

&/so, having journeyed too far to still be
complete fools, we sense, in our aspiration,
which way the all A-MERICAN breeze, sweet with
patriotic anthems blows, lufting the wee flags
as the floats roll by, like a procession of the
promises o'er the rainbow, Umph! Umph! Umph! Umph! For
no matter how we've been stamped: wop, ruskie, kike, kraut,
polack, frog, paddy, bohunk, Tramp! Tramp! Tramp! Tramp! we
think we've been taught by Minstrelsy, God the Father
& Mother Nature's natural selection, our
skin tone is the least beastly.

RASTUS:

They pray complexion will negate their rejection,
Tramp! Tramp! That their non-black pigmentation will prove
a springboard, ace, saving grace & passageway
to the devoutly to be desired FREE WHITE
PERSONHOOD, the ultimate firewall
separating them from *"them."* (Us.)

MICK:

We labor to hitch our wagon to the A-
MERICAN star, re-cast(e) ourselves, by sopping up
its customs & notions like sun soaked quilts airing
on tenement fire escapes or homestead fences.
We're tutored to bend, blend, be bland.

RASTUS:

& as their reward (Doodah) our aspirant
antagonists get to toe-dip in the mainstream
of deliverance & self-esteem, a preamble
to wrapping their troubles in the fundamental
& fundamentalist scheme of the All A-
MERICAN dream.

MICK:

& in continued pursuit of The Big Promise
of material, social & emotional
liberty, we pledge our allegiance, oppose
abolition &, from that platform, our first
privileged position, laugh the laugh of patriots
at the fun, poked (Hah Hah) with poisoned pike at their
mocked black opposition.

Doors open at 6, curtain at 7 fifteen.

See
on stage,
"A BREATH OF AIR FROM THE SUNNY SOUTH."
a dreamy backdrop of the dear ol' Sweet Southland,
fancied realm of milk & honey. Quixotic.
Bucolic. Sublime. Serene. Hear the strains of the
banjo, trombone, fiddle & tambourine.
"SPLENDID SCENERY AND HANDSOME COSTUMES"
Enter Mr. Interlocutor, like the Doctor
in the *commedia dell'arte* (nudge nudge).
The haughty M.C. straightman stands between, followed

by a march of minstrels. Lawd a'mussy. The
common black & the black common experience.
Coons as they really is. See their blackened faces
with white eyes saucer-sized & watermelon grins
from (y)ear to (y)ear. Lawd a'mussy, look-a' dem coons!
Yass, yass. Togged in pied Harlequin-like livery
of paint box gaudy cast offs & hand-me-down rigs
fit only for nigs, parading about the stage
all a-fidget & a-jitter, a-spasm &
a-twitch, & a-singing & a-high kicking all
the while.
     Look at 'em! Coons on the hoof! (Hah! Hah!)
as they sho nuff natchul is. Frolicking, frisky
cavorters, scruffy footwear aflop & swallow-
tailed frocks a-drag behind 'em, with buttons 'bout
the size of banjo bottoms. Look at 'em, *Lawdy*,
Lawdy, coons hardly able to contain their delight
at (Hah Hah) being coons.

BROTHER BONES: Boy, you one nigga is sho got a ear for music!
BROTHER TAMBO: Boy, you is right, *"A ear for music"* is sho nuff
                what I got!
BROTHER BONES: Boy, you is one nigga is got a foot for dancing!
BROTHER TAMBO: Boy, you is sho right, *"A foot for dancing"* is sho
        nuff is what I got! And you know what else I is got?
BROTHER TAMBO: Tell me, what else you is sho got, Brother Bones.
BROTHER BONES: Well, I is sho got me a mouth for watermelons
               'n' po'k chops!

RASTUS:
Followed by snorts & sniggers, cackles & titters;
gales of tee-hees, ha-has, ho-hos & hee-hees,
breeding a slew of aisle rolling, knee slapping, pants
peeing fit-to-bust aspirant onlookers laughing
theyselves ill. Twill by 'n' by, Mr. Interlocutor
calls for order in lingo as extravagantly
embroidered in its parody of highbred

pomposity as the Minstrel's hand-basted
mockery of the enslaved's threadbare servility.
But it's all six & two threes to the huddled-muddle's
green redwhite&blue ears. What each hears sounds side
splittingly & factual & actual as spun gold.

PADDY:
(Third from the end)
"Gentlemen, be seated!" & a-seated we be,
aplop in a semicircle of wiggling,
wriggling, gag-pulling, gobbledygook-gabbling
plantation puppies, anchored on the ends by
Brudders Tambo & Bones. Led by ringmaster &
brains with the reins, Mr. Interlocutor.

MICK:
(In the cheap seats)
He's in charge, we think, Mr. Interlocutor.
Him. His Nibs is most like us,
except for his longhairs'-like fusty airs, we
(proudly) fit the bill: low-brow, no-brow. Run of the mill.
Common as swill. Anti-frill. It's the cut of his
egghead jib makes him, not us, the butt of their
caper cutting, their skits & jibes & jester gestures.
Yes (Hah Hah) him, Lord Muck, not us.

PADDY:
Hear me croon, in sentimental tenor, a sweet,
pro-slavery ballad heralding *"A Dream of
the Southland,"* the joyous plantation life
'midst the camp grounds & cotton fields down home,

"REPLETE WITH COMEDY AND PATHOS
AND MINGLING WITH TEARS IN A
MOST MARVELOUS FASHION"

MICK:
Delivers it so tuggingly at the heartstrings

we all A-MERICAN common Men consumers
wish we could be slaves too. *"My golly, what a show!"*
as the minstrels chant the chants*:*   *"Wheel*

> *about*
>
> *turn about,*
>
> *do jes*
>
> *so. Wheel*
>
> *about*
>
> *turn*
>
> *about,*
>
> *do jes*
>
> *so."*

A rousing rockin' de heel, hoe-down finale.
The Olio.

RASTUS:

See, in the trance of their *mental imperceptiveness*,
the imitator's, the missionary minstrels,
zombie-like dance —*like one induced by another*—
that, venturing, *in their highly suggestive state*,
into the unexplored dark territory of,
they think, in the . . . *impassivity* . . . of un-
intelligence . . . of their disowned selves' . . . *moral
insensibility* . . . simple signifying —
or Signifyin(g), as some would have it —version
of, as legend would have it, a crippled
"Ethiopian's" natural coon carryings on,
but is really, to begin with, a mocking by
said darkie of the staid (near 'bout daid) ballroom dances
done by their owners, or, equally sly & wily,
a looselimbed, double dupe cameo of low class
Irish whirligig jigs, but, when all turned about
& wheeled about, climaxed in the blackened white
faced delineators canter & shout (as if
they really know what it's all about) Ha Ha,
speaking in flat talkin' coonese tongues, as they
"Wheel about turn about do

jes so."
See the imposters knocked crazy, dancing the dance,
arms & legs akimbo, heads a-bob on their
looseygoosey necks
"and
every time
I wheel about,"
eyes rolling in their sockets like crapshooter's bones.
"I jump Jim Crow!"

Stuff

like that, plus a hogshead of other self-
deflating Hah hahs & zippidy-coon doodahs.

MICK:
Golly, what a show! & its message is loud & clear!
& simple as pie: "Coons is buffoons." A message
that will guide us new common Man A-MERICAN
consumers through our Theology of The Rising
Race, "Coons is buffoons, & we ain't!" Yas yas.
A message so plain & powerful & timely &
primary it immediately possesses
the whole, the soul, the psyche of All A-merica.
A dollar for dolor truth. Based at base, on the
self-congratulatory belief in the All
A-MERICAN notion of "Our" enterprise, our
pluck. Our God blessed bread earned by the sweat of our
Industrious brow, vs. "their" idleness. Isn't
seeing believing? See the indolent darkies
blissful in their Edenic ignorance. Nigh
electric in its eclectic vim. See them dance,
sing.
      "BRIGHT NEW SONGS."
                    See them frisk &
frolic with nar' a care, letting the devil take
the middling & fiddling hindmost, whilst *we* true

aspiring redwhite&blue all A-MERICANs
in honest toil are prudent, diligent, staunch.
We do jes so, slogging grudgingly along, *ONE*,
2, *THREE*, 4 at this petty pace, day to day, sound,
full of fury, shoulders turned jes so to the grindstone,
noses to the . . . wheel
about
turn about, an' do
jes

   so . . . Not being "them" helps to make us us.
That, in part, is part of what they're for.

RASTUS:
Therefore this "truth" is held to be self-evident
& feeds a need & is adopted with giddy speed
& is instantly integrated (nudge nudge)
into the mainstream average everyday Public
Consciousness of the New common Man aspirant
A-MERICAN consumers as The Truth.

MICK:
IT IS DELIGHTFUL . . .
The Whole Truth,
"WONDERFUL
INSTRUCTIVE AND MORAL"
& nothing but, so help us God.

Coons is buffoons.

WELBOURNE:
What *is* it, w*hat* is it about the White Negro
Minstrel entertainment experience (for
perpetrators & consumers)?

MICK:
It's the performer's rebuking of our, their
fellow aspirants', fears. Their stepping forth from, to

quote John Quincy Adams, a *"motley rabble of saucy boys, negroes & mulattoes, Irish teagues & outlandish jack tarrs."* It's the revolutionary act called for by revolutionary times. The Boston Tea Party in our war of independence.

RASTUS:
The opening raid, in the all A-MERICAN tradition of slippin' 'cross the line disguised in BLACK FACE.

CHAPTER

6

 A Middle Passage, or Bridge

Traversed by Frederick Douglass,

William Henry Lane, and a Sense of the

Increased Speed of Things

1843–1848

VOICE OF THE BLACK EYE:

&,

1843: Witnesses the first Christmas card & "A Christmas Carol" by Charles Dickens, short stories by Edgar Allen Poe. *"Columbia, the Gem of the Ocean (Columbia the Land of the Brave)"* is the day's popular musical favorite.

& then one fine morning some time around about then, the Worker is a-wakened by a hiss, clack & rumble. Passing him by is a parade of new fangled doohickeys & hickeymadoos.

"Chirographer" (a.k.a. type-writer), the first long distance telegraph wire, strung between Baltimore & D.C., the Howe Sewing Machine. & The Worker looks up & every-thing begins to accelerate 2, 3, 4. 123412341234 until its like Little Black Sambo hotfooting it from the tiger. But, instead of The Worker's Time melting like butter it multiplies, till it's on all The Worker's hands, & it takes some newfangled doohickey or hickeymadoo or new amusement to kill it.

Cross cut:

RASTUS:
Abolitionists scold & sermonize, minstrels
entertain.

VOICE OF THE BLACK EYE:
& so it'll be so forth & so on,
&/so for the next decade or so, amusement & science, minstrels &
manumission,
symbolized by Darwin sailing the oceans blue, collecting wildlife
specimens: fauna & fossils to systemize,
& Barnum, assailing the notions of true, projecting life's wild
specimens: freaks & fascinations, to tantalize, each applying the
principle of THOMAS ROBERT MALTHUS, English parson
Malthus (1766–1834) said industrialized society's incomes outpace
population growth, which out-pace food production, which proves
war, plagues, slavery & infanticide are all good for the stimulation of
more Industry & the discouragement of indolence,

Doodah.
So, the finest, the fittest (& most foul, I might add) Succeed, Malthus
reasons,
& the ordinary & hindmost gush in a rush like slush from a busted
barrel's bottom, Ha ha.

Cross cut:

RASTUS:
Abolitionists scold & sermonize, minstrels entertain.

PADDY:
& the form solidifies itself.

VOICE OF THE BLACK EYE:
& in
1844. *"Buffalo Girls (Won't You Come Out Tonight?)"*
by the pseudonymous *"Cool White"* (nudge nudge) is a hit.

A newly patented 6-shooter comes out & a handful of Texas Rangers use it to bump off 150 *Comanch.*

"What," the first message sent by telegraph wire asks, *"hath God Wrought!"*

The YMCA is founded in London. Barnum's American Museum continues to pull them in. A wood pulp process produces paper cheap enough to print pap to placate the mass, the pawns, moving forward 1 square at a time.

"All for one & one for all," cry the heroes of African-French novelist Alexandre Dumas' (1802–1870) *The Three Musketeers.*

RASTUS:
Meanwhile, abolitionists scold & sermonize;
minstrels entertain.

EYE OF THE BLACK VOICE:
& in
1845 machinery improvements of every sort multiplied like rabbits: raw cotton & wool are mechanically combed; steam pumps down, becomes compound, wheels around & around, spins out hydroelectricity, power from running water, splish splash; work goes faster & faster till the workers huff & puff, their eyes spinning like Barney Google's bonging & bugging at the lurid illustrations in *The Police Gazette,* that scandalous rag.

& James O. Andrews has slaves. There are objections. Serious ones. Andrews is a bishop of the Methodist Episcopalian Church.
Bishop: Middle English, from Old English *bisceope,* from Vulgar Latin **ebiscopus,* from Late Latin *episcopus,* from Late Greek *episkopos,* from Greek, overseer: *epi-,* epi- + *skopos,* watcher.

"**1.** A spiritual superintendent or overseer in the Christian Church." The Methodist Episcopalian Church splits into northern & southern blocs. Bishop Anderson, in his burgundy rig, maneuvers diagonally

across unoccupied spaces, keeps his slaves
(did you note the "overseer" in the definition above?)
& his Bishop's gig.
Doodah.
& Florida becomes the 27th state, & the U.S. gets dibs on the
Republic of Texas. It annexes it from Mexico. Mexico cries foul. War
ensues. The 267,338 square miles become the 28th state. Friendship
is its Motto. Friendship, remember, is Amistad in Spanish.
The mockingbird, Florida's state bird, is gray
& white. Its M.O. is aping the songs of other
birds. It, therefore, is the avian equivalent
of the Minstrel.
Doodah.

RASTUS:
In that same year, & coincidentally or not,
the *Knickerbocker Magazine* asks, *"Who
are our true rulers?"* In its wisdom, or audacity,
& in one fell swoop, condemning the majority's
methods & motives, lays it out thusly:
"The Negro poets, to be sure."

Then, in one fell swoop, knock & mock the reality of the minstrel
mentality, both methods & motives, putting it, à la *Jeopardy*, in the
form of a question, rhetorical though it may be: "Do they not set the
fashion, and give laws to the public taste? Let one of them, in the
swamps of Carolina, compose a new song, and it no sooner reaches
the ear of a white amateur, than it is written down, amended (that
is, almost spoilt), printed, and then put upon a course of rapid
dissemination, to cease only with the utmost bounds of Anglo-
Saxondom, perhaps with the world. Meanwhile, the poor author digs
away with his hoe, utterly ignorant of his greatness."

This as Andrew Jackson, *"one of the people,"* hero
of the common man, croaks. Jackson, wills his mansion
"with the negroes and all else on it," to a
nephew adopted as his son. Doodah.

VOICE OF THE BLACK EYE:
1846–1847
& in the new thing of schemes
speed being time & time being money
the flatbed press (print, flip, print, flip)
is made moot by (1812–1886) Richard Hoe's
rotary method (spin around spin around),
printing the page's 2 faces 10,000 per hour,
making more pap for the masses possible.
It is pure *"lightning."* Not to be confused with Lightnin',
the devilishly slow (shuffle, stop, shuffle, stop) janitor
at the Mystic Knights of the Sea Lodge,
dodge of those next-century bogus-colored cullions
Amos & Andy.
Lightnin', rendered on TV by Horace Stewart, a.k.a.
Nick O'Demus,
Bre'r Rabbit's voice in "The Song of the South,"
Disney's adaptation of Joel Chandler Harris'
Uncle Remus appropriations of African folk tales,
the first stories child Walt, Zip-a-Dee-Doo-Dah,
ever read.
Stewart's portrayal was lode from the Minstrelsy mine,
like lead from the Winnebago, Meskwaki &
Sauk Indian territories in Iowa,
which became in '46 the 29th state.
Most of the balls that slew & maimed
from the barrels of colonialists' muskets
were molded from Iowa ore.
& the popular tune of the Doodah Da day,
Jim Crack Corn.

RASTUS:
(Correcting)
Gimcrack corn! & not just catchy ditty for
the Dick & Jane set, a self-congratulatory
drinking song speaking across death's chasm, a true
two faced bit of blank faced sarcasm. Permit me

to slide some subtext up under it: A black
menial's corn likker'd lament following his
owner's accident.

OL' JOHN:
(Surviving member of that owner-slave duo)
To my horror & surprise, ol' massa, a kindly gent in my humble eyes,
being bucked (flip flop) to his untimely demise, when an unshooed
blue tail fly nipped his pony about its thigh. Even to the most diligent
shooer, like yours truly, the law of average does apply, perhaps
unduly; one can only fan so many of them bloodsucking dipterous
aphids of the family Tabanidae, before one does what that one did.
Causing massa's stallion to rear & jump, trying to beat a retreat, & ol'
massa go bump, head first at my unshod feet. So though good massa's
been heaven sent, wasn't me boss, I'm innocent. Don't embroil me in
that embrigglement; the only villain I can surmise is that pesky bug,
so, all Ol' John's got to say
is Doodah & pass the jug.
(Singing, slurred)
Jim crack corn — I don't care,
Old Massa gone away.

RASTUS:
Bugs, that Wabbit with suspiciously African-
like trickster traits, sang his own Looney Tunes version.
What's up, Doc?

MICK:
The English repeal the Corn Law;
say No More to Irish imports.

MARX:
(Reading from his *Communist Manifesto*)
"The proletarians have nothing to lose but their chains,"

MICK:
. . . & our place & dignity. In Erin we're called

cottiers *("peasants who live in cottages")*,
are told, by absentee land lords, to get the lead
& our sorry Irish arses off from their tenant
plot parcels.

ABSENTEE LANDLORD:
Way must be made for the more profitable cattle rising.

MICK:
A 4-year potato famine follows. *"Nothing
to lose but our chains,"* my bleeding Irish arse.

ABSENTEE LANDLORD:
It isn't so much that yes, they had no potatoes,
we English, by Divine Providence get first dibs.
& trade would be hurt if we sent relief.

MICK:
Uncle Sam ships a million dollars' worth of aid.

ABSENTEE LANDLORD:
But, lo, the lowly Irish lack the means to haul
the bounty home, where they've no ovens to bake bread
from the grain, even if they could.

MICK:
Near a million Irish starve.

WELBOURNE & RASTUS & PADDY:
Another 1.6 million
immigrate to the U.S.

RASTUS:
&, yes, the family of 87 emigrants of the Donner Party wagon
training for California, 3 months snowtrapped in the Sierra Nevada,
have no potatoes. A cannibalistic dinner party ensues. 46 survive. &
round donuts, cheap tin cans & sticky back postage stamps arrive,

& Cartier, Louis Francois, opens a petite jewelry shop in Paris, &
Liberia is founded in Africa to send free U.S. blacks back where they
were free in the first place, & the 5 year old *"New York game"* finds its
form & establishes its rules & has its season. Batter up!

VOICE OF THE BLACK EYE:

& 1847

Close up: Frederick Douglass (1818?–1895). Orator, Abolitionist,
former slave, sits for his portrait.
The photographer, under the velvet drape,
hides from the inverted eyes, agate-hard &
looking through the box's lens, seeing,
through the shutter & plate, down the bellows & through
him & the hand writing on the wall & beyond.
He does not implore the negro to smile. Hand
trembling, releases the shutter. Snap. Douglass holds,
does not blink.
Bushfire mane. Plow rutted brow. Broad
nostril'd. Lips a thin gash through beard.

Montage: British friends purchase his freedom.
Founds the abolitionist paper the *North Star.*
North Star. Celestial point for northward navigation.
End jewel in Little Dipper "handle";
in ancient times Ursa Minor was the *Dragon's wing.*
Fly away! Fly away! Follow the North Star, *Fly away!*
The North Star. "Right is of no Sex—Truth is of no Color—
God is the Father of us all, and we are all brethren,"
is its motto.

Douglass exits the Orpheum having seen his first minstrel show.
The laughter a wasp in his ear. He holds the programme rolled like

a switch. Striding rapidly toward the Assembly Hall. A passerby
speaks. He does not hear them but he nods.
We see him now in slow motion. Like he is wading, knee deep against
the current, eyes keen, fixed.

THIS EVENING
FREDERICK DOUGLASS
Lecture to commence at ½ past 7

The *North Star* is a stick. A big stick assault on slavery's aspects
& forms. Swagger stick. Carrot & stick of promised recompense
& threat. A goad, prod & pike to hasten the day of universal
emancipation for the 3 million still in slavery. A jackstraw, a wand.
Each edition, column & line is a crabstick, linstock, a staff promoting
the moral & intellectual improvement of (faceless) colored people.
It is a bail, a baton, a single stick. A switch. Raising welts on Jim
Crow's buttocks.
Leaning forward, arms straight as rails; fingers talons on the oak
podium, he reads them, sitting stern, earnest. Clinch mouthed,
foreheads rucked like washboards.
Solemn as stele.
Trying to summon up a song, gurgle & hock it up like phlegm, a
spirit-song—of the harmony of their labor—so he can spit it out
at them—a jigging song—a song of gladness in the task—of the
depth of the evil & foolishness flaming all around them—with a high
stepping melody for strides with a kick at the end of each one—for
crossing all lines & boundaries. His fist about to clinch, rise, elbow
bent, to beat, like a drumstick against the Meeting Hall air, thick as
cotton lint,
2, 3, 4!
Douglass, essayist, autobiographer, is proof coloreds ought have
more than aught voice in their emancipation. He, future counselor to
Lincoln & ambassador to Haiti, in a last minute change announces
Minstrelsy as his topic. He brands it an entertainment which holds
"up to ridicule an already too much oppressed people." Its perpetrators he

nails as "filthy scum," who pretend their foolish representations
"are the characteristics of the whole people." Psalms 92:3'7 his text,
its cadence is its context. Not for their lack of loving kindness, but
their failure of acknowledgment or penance he hews into them like a
chorus of whet-edged axes into punk wood.
The collection plates brimmed to overflowing.

RASTUS:
The blackened faced en-actors & the bulk of their
"working 'class'" public, want—without wait or weight—want
to *Be* & to consume, to glut, like wakened bears
stumbling ravenous into cold sunlight of spring slush,
to grab & gobble purple pawed, juice jawed, smacking
& slurping at a berry bush in the grove of
FREE WHITE PERSONHOOD, to sate a hunger whet
by the hibernation of their long winter of
banishment & discontent.

VOICE OF THE BLACK EYE:
Hibernating bears maintain bones & muscle mass by not excreting,
but recycling bodily wastes.
Craft your own analogies.

&/so, in '47 another counter-
acting propagation ensues against notions
of propriety & possibility when
William Henry Lane (circa 1825?–
1853?) an African American
under the cover of darkness (nudge . . .) joins the Ethiopian
Serenaders, the nation's
#1 BLACKENED FACED MINSTRELSY TROUPE
A wonder indeed & by deed, Lane becomes
a boggleboe & as big a hoax as Barnum's Joice Heth.
Bigger perhaps. For when Lane, as "Master Juba,
THE DANCING WONDER OF THE AGE"
passes (. . . nudge) himself off as a truly
authentic white blackened faced imitation black

& is proclaimed no less than the best of his
blackened faced ilk by no less than novelist
Charles Dickens (1812–1870).

Dickens, the most popular novelist of his day, knew, perhaps,
metaphorically of which he spoke. Humiliated as a child hireling in
an English blacking factory, causing, some think, dark matter in the
form of shadowy Doppelgangers to later dance like Jubas through
a Dickens tale or 2 (e.g., *Great Expectations*, *Little Dorrit* & *David
Copperfield*, to name a few). These darkened doubles, served, like
ablutions, in another Jonson's, Ben's (no relation) *Black Masque*'s
Britannia waters, washing away the psychic blight of their past, so
they could forget their troubles, get on board, get happy & sail away
to the Promised Land flowing with milk & honey & Free White
Personhood. Doodah.
&/so Lane *"Dancinest fellow ever was"*
in his gimmicking mime & capering steps:
"Single shuffle, double shuffle, cut and cross-cut,"
was smack dab in the tradition of counter-
vailing underdog: a truly authentic black
blackened faced imitator doing a
disguised about face intimation of a white
blackened faced imitator imitating a
truly (in)authentic black. & in the doing,
Lane truly tips the top, flips the flop, slips the slop,
cops a swap, ego trips & 1-upmanships at
1 & the same mimicking time, wheeling about,
turning about
&,
in the doing
just so,
with a ringtailed, strictly taboo coup

of subversive derring-do,
jumps
Jim
Crow
&
in the doing,
works an unannounced & un-
beknownst switcheroo breakthrough: a blackened
black face facing an audience of white
aspiring free whites &
in the doing,
disappears without ever being visible,
or, as runaway slaves put it, stealing himself
back. & like Barnum's color-hanging novelty,
before their very eyes!

Frontal aside: Rice & the other MINSTRELs' crossovers paled
by comparison
(nudge nudge). Mirror, mirror on the wall, who's the fairest . . .
One wonders, that's all. But, alas, 1 blackbird does not a spring
make. (Doodah.) Blackened faced minstrels can't flock to the stage
until after the so-called Emancipation—almost 2 decades away, three,
4. . . .

1848,
California here they come—bum rushing the latest discovery: Gold!
1848,
John Quincy Adams suffers a stroke. Mustard plasters & leech
bleeding are administered. *"This is the end of the earth, but I am
composed,"* he says, & dies.

CHAPTER

7

 Daddy Rice

Runs the Doo Doo Down

Harriet Beecher Stowe and John Brown

Turn Up the Heat

1848–1870

———•◦•———

"The two most popular characters in the world are [Queen] Victoria
[1819–1901] and the famed Jim Crow," the *Boston Post* editorializes.

One might, still, in the face of scholarly &
latter day commiserator's apologetic
spinning & grinning, be left to wonder: was it
Rice's notion merely to entertain? Is it simply
Irish luck? Is he just a blackened faced
white performance artist trying to make a buck?
(Nudge nudge). Just a *"delineator"*? doing mild
debunkings of the "antics & repartee"
of the enslaved? Or, was Douglass on to something?
Was Rice up to something? Were there other, fine print
items, on Daddy's Minstrel agenda?

            Entering
into the record the subject's own words, spoken
some years hence:

RICE:

*"I effectually proved that negroes are
essentially an inferior species
of the human family and they ought to
remain slaves."*

VOICE OF THE BLACK EYE:

He continues, declaiming the fluff of legends
Of his portrayal as,

RICE:

*"a fair representative of the great body
of our slaves."*

VOICE OF THE BLACK EYE:

That recognition, he concludes, will,

RICE:

*"ever be a source of pride to me that in my
humble line, I have been of such signal service
to my country."*

VOICE OF THE BLACK EYE:

Doodah & Hurrah Hurrah. Clear enough? Hands;
any doubts 'bout MINSTRELSY'S intent? Any wonder
as to
its course?

Take it as the opening statement, as it were,
of the notion of A-MERICAN Black Face

Minstrelsy.

Rice & the attitude that fueled the blackened faced
faux foolishness (nudge nudge) was not a show of love
for his fellows in affliction down on the ground.

RICE:

If we must pilfer from the house of our neighbor
& signify falsely in the marketplace
of entertainment, forgive us, but it was salt
for our soup, wine for our flagons. If, beneath the
banner of minstrelsy we blackened-faced gathered
our people together as under the cover of darkness . . .

VOICE OF THE BLACK EYE:

Doodah.

RICE:

. . . like thieves in the night . . .

VOICE OF THE BLACK EYE:

Nudge nudge.

RICE:

& went out to escape the inequity, then
trespass or transgression was the price
of the ticket. We Minstrels were as Moses,
leading the parade of the hope-to-be-respectables
with hardened hearts, crossing the great divide & burning
our bridges as they went.

VOICE OF THE BLACK EYE:

&
so,
behold the message of the words & ways
of MINSTRELSY, saying, *"Yea, slavery is good*
& good for them." & that message came unto the
South & all concerned, saying, *"Ye that tremble at*
the threat of change, neither fear
nor let your hearts feel faint. & furthermore,"
say the words & ways of
MINSTRELSY, *"the most deservedly un-*
deserving down in Dixie darkies are humble,

superstitious, homespun, sub-human, Faithful Souls,
as happy in vassalage (Hah Hah) as sows in slop,
as content as lambs in clover."
                                    & thus, contends
a close reading between the lines of the words &
ways of MINSTRELSY,
          "Fret not friends & fellow A-
MERICANs. Nothing to fear but fear itself. &
furthermore," say the words & ways of MINSTRELSY,
"as for them Northern freedmen? well, them cheeky rascals, them uppity sables,
with their insolent airs,
sissy ways, dandy faux fop fashions & fractured
declension (Hah Hah) are too busy failing
at being White Men to matter." (A

notion [Hah
Hah]
at least as old as Shakespeare
[William, 1564–1616]. Black
faced portrayals
& betrayals
& all that. See that fellow
Othello
[with his good name flinched]:
Othello: Moor
as less;
seen by some
as a forewarning,
a signification to white girl's daddies;
might wake up one morning
& one'll've gotten way too big
& much too close.
"You'll have your daughter cover'd with a Barbary horse,
you'll have your nephews neigh to you,"

that is to say to you, Othello, he be
chump-meat

for the carpetbagger wily ego
of I-
ago.)

RICE:
Forget all about 'em. Let the South (Hear! hear!)
take care of its own" (Hee Hee) say the words & ways
of MINSTRELSY, *"On with the show!"* (Hah Hah).

VOICE OF THE BLACK EYE:
&/so,
MINSTRELSY, the All A-MERICAN
"entertainment," "the genuine show, the
extravagant nigger show," as American
writer & humorist Mark Twain (1835–
1910) enthuses, is custom Procrustean
cut for the common man & the aspiring
A-MERICAN consumers. It is the gauge,
the guiding light, the archetype, the very model
of a modern & mighty amusement, fit for
their devoutly desired admission into
FREE WHITE PERSONHOOD.

&/so,
to the tea totaling, anti-immigrant
excluders MINSTRELSY is the paradigmatic
form of counter indoctrination to the
fanatical Abolitionists' cry for
Emancipation. Thus, while riding the crest
of its approval, MINSTRELSY, like post-flood water
in lust of the lowest level,
       trickles
       down
to kowtow to the unsung, true, red white & blue
no brow, bottom rung, foreign or base born, but
aspiring all A-MERICAN consumer
(who, at a performance, can [according to the
A-MERICAN Dream] fear no evil, embarrassment,

vexation, intimidation, or spleen &
"get it," with even half a wit, see what I mean?).

& where, you ask, is God in this scheme of things?

THE ASPIRING TO FREE WHITE PERSONHOOD:
(With a sigh)
God is omnipotent, God is infinite, God
is transcendent. & God is on our side.
Hasn't He provided for body & soul.
Hasn't He, in His Generosity, given us
bountiful A-MERICA? Doesn't that prove His
mercy. Doesn't that prove His compassion. Doesn't
that prove His justice & judgment & approval
of our plan, process & progress. Yes. & His truth
is in our self-evident marching on, *ONE*, 2,
THREE, 4.

VOICE OF THE BLACK EYE:
&/so, taking commonality of intent
as sanction & with bless'd assurance as license
& without seeming conscience or unseemly
consequence, it is on with the show they go;
the Emerald Isle sons of ingress, grappling &
grabbling against we blacks with whom they wallow
in the common dross, scrambling to rise above this muck,
& march toward the Elysium of FREE WHITE
PERSONHOOD, groping their way, Stamp! Stamp!
jovially singing.

THE ASPIRING:
(Roused)
*"O'er their black backs we go, b'hoys! (Hah Hah), O'er their
backs we go! (Ho Ho),"*

VOICE OF THE BLACK EYE:
2, *THREE*, 4.

That's entertainment & pontificating
Minstrelsy style, while abolitionists, rock-stern,
pinched, dust-dry, scold & sermonize,
& the Republic edges ever forward
toward the combustible culmination
of the failure to set boundaries & the testing
of the endurance of opposing social,
political, economic & governmental forms.

& in his allegorical **1851**
ragtag ragtime tome with Minstrel-like metaphors
on retribution Herman Melville (18-
19–1891) riffed on the meditations of
maniacal men in pursuit of an all powerful whiteness:
"I protested my innocence of these things. I saw
that under the mask of these half humorous
innuendoes . . . was full of his insular prejudices."
& a little deeper in, Ahab, obsessed with the symbol of whiteness,
concludes, *"All visible objects, men, are but as pasteboard masks.*
But in each event —in the living act, the undoubted deed
—there some unknown but still reasoning thing
puts forth the mouldings of its features from behind
the unreasoning mask. If man will strike through the mask!
How can the prisoner reach outside
except by thrusting through the wall?"
How, Ahab? How
indeed.

EYE OF THE BLACK VOICE:
Then,
in '52 *Uncle Tom's Cabin*, penned by
Harriet Beecher Stowe
(1811–1896),
"The Lady Who Did Her Own Work,"
& whose husband, Calvin E., haled from South Natick, Mass.,
site of enslavement of Crispus Attucks,
"the first to defy, the first to die" in the A-merican War of Independence,

is published. Harriet despised the notions of slavery & store-bought bread,
peopled *Cabin* with the likes of Little Eva & Uncle Tom,
the former, the kindest, lovingest little mistress (as in owner)
any vassal could ever hope to have, or weep over in death
(nudge nudge) & the latter, faithful, pious Uncle Tom,
a slave master's ideal, who, during his curtain speech,
prays not for his own soul, but that his owner,
who has beaten him almost to death, will repent
& be saved, out Poitiering Poitier at the end of *The Defiant Ones*,
eleven decades later. Gorged with the gospel of slavery's perversions,
overnight the book becomes the abolitionist's diversionary rebuttal,
a 2 edged sword, a treat & threat. It amuses & forces awareness,
forges opinion & finally confrontation.

ABE LINCOLN:
(Meeting Harriet Beecher Stowe)
"So, you are the little woman who wrote the book
that started this great war!"

VOICE OF THE BLACK EYE:
'Tis in 1857
Uncle Tom's Cabin takes to the stage like swine to swill.
Troupes of *"Tom shows"* by the score crusade to & through every sector,
nook, nest, corner & cranny, in every alcove and at every cross-roads,
among every aggregation & accumulation urban, rural & in between,
in halls (assembly, lecture & convention) & lyceums &
auditoria, wagon backs, river boats, dime museums,
theaters, playhouses, opera houses, arenas & town squares,
tents & orchards & barren fields. Over the next couple decades it is seen
by more than the total population of A-MERICA.

HARRIET B. S.:
(Discoursing on negroes as she reads from Dred)
*"abundant animal nature . . . if they ever
become highly civilized, they will excel in music,*

dancing and elocution," in that *"department*
which lies between the sensuousness and the
intellectual—what we call the elegant arts."

VOICE OF THE BLACK EYE:
How's that for looking the gift horse in the mouth &
calling the golden egg a spade? Doodah, Drum DRUM.
But, A-MERICAN black faced Minstrelsy, being
stronger than Truth or fiction, changes the face &
motive of Stowe's novel undertaking.
The declamatory, pasteboardy makeup
of her cast, bunkuming & jabbering up
for the stage, magnified the clichés & minimized
her message & intent. How's that for irony.
& how about this: during *Tom's* stage runs, the Dixie
whistling Supreme Court, in its Legree-like decree,
stamp! stamp! stamp! stamps! stamp! stamp! stamps!
7 to 2 against the suit filed by (he
argued) former slave Dred Scott (née Sam Blow) (c.
1795–1858)
ringing down the curtain on notions
of the Compromise, allowing Missouri
to enter the Union as a slave state & Maine
as a free state & declaring the Constitution
never had the *"unhappy black race"* in mind,
ruling there's no escape clause there. Not only
isn't Scott free, he, nor any other slave is
not, nor can they ever a citizen be, of
any of the states or federal territories.
Hip hip say slave holders, Boo Hoo & Hup hup, 3,
4, say abolitionists. See the divide widen.

EYE OF THE BLACK VOICE:
See Northern Republicans & Southern Democrats
shake like Minstrels' dry bones, hear them rattle their sabers,
shout "We must RULE!" Hear the sound of the seismic split
(Drum DRUM) running roughly along the Mason-Dixon,

down the Mississippi down to New Orleans. (Drum DRUM)
Hear the muffled bowbowbows of the hell-hounds of war.
Hear soundings of the bugle's alarm,
the under rumbling rat a tat tats of martial drumtaps,

HUP, 2, as they rally 'round, hurrah *THREE*, 4,
come to order (DRUM drum) strike up the band,
& continue marching (DRUM drum) for-
ward marching as to war. (Drum DRUM)

VOICE OF THE BLACK EYE:
In **1859**
Drum DRUM, Drum DRUM, the African Squadron, an A-
MERICAN fleet restraining slave trade from Africa's
west, is called back to enforce a blockade ag'in'
the South.
Drum DRUM. Drum DRUM.
Making abolitionist an active verb,
John Brown (1800–1859), God's anti-
slavery saber, heading a rag tag army
of 21 blacks & whites, men & boys, captures
Harper's Ferry, a U.S. arsenal. Brown intends
to arm slaves, intends they will rise & by force
free themselves. Robert E. Lee (1807–
1870), leading the marine charge retakes
the armory. Brown, Drum DRUM Drum DRUM "his truth
marching on" DRUM Drum is tried for treason. Hung.
Drum DRUM. Harriet Ross Tubman (1820?–
1913), a Brown co-conspirator, was
ill & missed the raid. She weeps over his death, then,
like a true trooper, she sees to it that the show
goes on. A slavery escapee she'd returned
from whence she'd fled to abscond
with 300 bondsmen & bondsmaids who dwelt &
labored in the valley of the Dixie shadow,
returned through the scent of magnolias to diminish
& defile the evil institution & beget

upheaval, returned to commit a sin worthy
of death, her capture worth 40 thousand in Con-
federate money. She jumped down, turned around, bailed
a picker of cotton. . . . Returned. Returned. Returned.
Returned. & returned. . . . During the war Tubman will
heal, spy & do laundry. Drum DRUM Drum Dah Dum.
1859, as Charles Dickens said in *A Tale of*
Two Cities, published that year, *"was the season of Light,*
it was the season of Darkness . . ."

EYE OF THE BLACK VOICE:
It was also a year of births, firsts & starts on
all fronts: killers, chain stores & the 33rd state:
Billy the Kid, A&P & Oregon;
waterways, commercial oil wells, food preservation;
Suez Canal, paraffin wax; lost land, novels
& sports: President James Buchanan seizes more
Indian land, *Our Nig* & *Ursula*, by
Harriet E. Adams Wilson & Maria
Fermina dos Reis, black & Brazilian
writers, intercollegiate baseball; pop songs &
operas: *Dixie*, performed by Emmett's Virginia
Minstrels, & *Un Ballo in Maschera*, Verdi's
the *Masked Ball*; electrical home incandescence
reins light & darkness: & *At the Piano* by
U.S. émigré artist James Abbott McNeill
Whistler: 2 figures, 1 black clad the
other in white, face each other across the block
of a piano (But, nudge nudge, note the tonal
harmony & subtle coloring).

VOICE OF THE BLACK EYE:
& finally in '59, the formation
of the Ku Klux Klan. Have mercy & Doodah Da.

EYE OF THE BLACK VOICE:
&, in a parable, with a moral yet to be determined, an Australian

imports 2 score & 4 rabbits, intending them for hunting fun. 6 years
& 2 hundred-thousand hare homicides later there are twice that many
still on the hop, endangering the home economy by depleting grass
supplies needed for sheep.

Supply your own analogy and moral.

VOICE OF THE BLACK EYE:

How 'bout everyone in their place, and leaving well
enough alone. Doodah.

EYE OF THE BLACK VOICE:

& possibly on a related aside, *Natural Selection, or the Preservation of
Favored Species in the Struggle for Life* by Charles Darwin, is published.
Dah Dum. It rattles notions of natural order, & possibly on an other
related note, A-MERICA makes motions t'ward civil war. DRUM
Drum. *"Historians,"* Konrad Lorenz says, *"will have to face the fact that
natural selection determined the evolution of cultures in the same manner as it
did that of species."* DRUM Drum Doodah. . . . This is repeated . . .

VOICE OF THE BLACK EYE:

Evolution t'wer'n't nothing new, Aristotle (384–322 B.C.), Greek
philosopher who tutored Alexander the Third, a.k.a. the Great
(356–323 B.C.), in natural sciences, metaphysics, politics, poetics,
comparative anatomy, empirical observation & logic. Alex 3 (ox-
headed perhaps) fails to grasp the notion of war's vulgarity, as'll
be put forth in English poet Lord Byron's (1788–1824) view as the
"brainspattering, wind-pipe-splitting art . . . 'The' hired assassin's trade," so
said fellow poet, Percy Bysshe Shelley (1792–1822). Thus, bestride
his steed Bucephalus (that could not be tamed until its shadow was
cast behind it), Alexander (striving to overcome his Macedonian
roots & become Greek) conquered all of Greece, Persia, Egypt &
India by age 33. Aristotle, ahead of the curve, dug the evolutionary
notion back in 335.

& in the wings, that notion was in motion. &
befitting the biogenetic law of war, in
ways characteristic of the evolution

of the species, DRUM Drum, a *mise-en-scène* of whispers,
winds, platforms, scaffolding & properties, were amassed,
for curtain rise. DRUM Drum, DRUM Drum.

EYE OF THE BLACK VOICE:
1860
–1861
"are the spring of hope . . . the winter of despair . . ."
Lincoln elected with 40% of the vote;
railroad & steamship industries thrive; cotton, corn,
newspapers, tobacco & can production are
up; *"Old Black Joe,"* by Stephen Foster, is popular;
milk is pasteurized; U.S. population rises;
Indian's numbers are down. *"We had everything*
before us, we had nothing before us," Dickens riffed
in his tale of *"Liberty, Equality,*
Fraternity," à la The French Revolution.
DRUM Drum. CHOP Chop!

CHAPTER

8

The Civil War

&

Beyond Back to Where We Began

And Notions of High & Low Culture;

Dividing to Conquer

186?–1871

VOICE OF THE BLACK EYE:
& it comes to pass that the North & the South
gather together their armies.

EYE OF THE BLACK VOICE:
See them don they now their blue & gray apparel.

VOICE OF THE BLACK EYE:
& go forth against their enemy. Hear the guns
boom & blood cry out. Hear the muffled DRUM drum DRUM
drum as they come to order, strike up the bands . . .
                    (DRUM
DRUM) & the land is rent in twain from the top
to the bottom, fields are bloodied, cities cremated . . .
& the rich get richer, the poor need more, & Time
& the Press & Church & State & the A-
MERICANists Forward March as the bands play on,
ONE, 2 *THREE*, 4. DRUM Drum

Lincoln, faced with a slavery condoning
Constitution, showed both his cheeks as he waffled,
wavered, wobbled & swayed, then, in a gambit to pulp
the heart of Dixie's *"black money,"* began, bit by
bit, smidgen by shred to liberate by law & ploy,
ploy & law, a politically correct chosen
few, more to wound the South than heal the enslaved;
lastly proclaiming the emancipation of kit,
kin & caboodle to fight & forever be free.
Abolitionists applauded.

THE CONFEDERACY:
(Panning the notion)
The fight's about the Union, not our niggers.

THE ENSLAVED:
(Eye the North Star. Flee.)

VOICE OF THE BLACK EYE:
Drum DRUM Drum DRUM.

EYE OF THE BLACK VOICE:
1863,
The year of the Emancipation Proclamation,
Buddy Bolden is born. He will lose his mind after picking up the
cornet during the bloom of the post-war brass band craze, but not
before forming the first jazz band.

FRANCOISE SAGAN, née QUOIREZ:
(1935–2004. French novelist.)
"Jazz music is an intensified feeling of non-chalance."

VOICE OF THE BLACK EYE:
*"It seems to me monstrous that anyone should
believe that the jazz rhythm expresses America,"*
harps uncool Isadora Duncan. *"Jazz rhythm
expresses the primitive savage."* She also declared,

"The only dance masters I could have were
Jean-Jacques Rousseau, Walt Whitman and Nietzsche."

EYE OF THE BLACK VOICE:
She, San Fran born (1878?–1927), revolutionary dancer,
social critic, progressive thinker, theorist,
advocate of the poetic spirit, inventoress of modern dance,
fitness guru . . .

VOICE OF THE BLACK EYE:
. . . thought jazz rhythm didn't express America
but expressed the *"primitive savage."*
Of Isadora, Teddy Roosevelt, who didn't know much about art,
but knew what he liked, said she seemed to him
"as innocent as a child dancing through the garden
in the morning sunshine and picking the beautiful flowers of her fantasy."
Was this, do you think, despite, or because of,
her reputation for near nude dancing?
Was the Bull Moose happy to see her
or was that a big stick he was carrying?

ISADORA:
(Robes a-rustle)
"We may not all break the Ten Commandments, but we
are certainly all capable of it. Within us lurks
the breaker of all laws, ready to spring out
at the first real opportunity."

VOICE OF THE BLACK EYE:
Isadora, you mean Like, Like, Like, primitive savages in,
in, in like the *Land of Opportunity*, perhaps?

RASTUS:

Was in her & she denied what it is for what it was.
Typical of the undetected in the infected.
Wrap itself around your throat—like, well—like, you know—

VOICE OF THE BLACK EYE:

We conclude our Isadora quotes with, *"The first*
essential in writing about anything is that
the writer should have no experience of the matter."

RASTUS:

Whoa, mama. Ignorant arrogance. Deadly.

VOICE OF THE BLACK EYE:

This & all of her strokes of wit were said or writ'
we must assume with that enviable but grating A-
Merican lack of the ironic.

EYE OF THE BLACK VOICE:
1863

Congress passes Stay Out Of The Army for $300. Law
is protested by New York's Irish immigrants, a.k.a. b'hoys,
Bowery Boys.

PADDY:

(Irish immigrant. Voice of **New York's Bowery Boys, a.k.a. B'Hoys**)
If abolitionists crave a cause, why not ours?
Emancipate us. We're closer in kind & care
than these baboon's cousins they seek to deslave.
The coloreds are fatter fed, warmer housed, finer
clothed than our malnourished, shanty quartered, ragged
arses. & who champions our cause? Why, WHY should WE,
"saucy boys . . . Irish teagues & outlandish jack tarrs,"
with no way to pay, why should WE, go to war o'er
"negroes & mulattoes," who, if free, will command
our smoke-Irish jobs?

VOICE OF THE BLACK EYE:
The ruffians rally, like savage primitives,
turn rabid, riot. A colored orphanage is
torched. For 3 bloodthirsty nights & Doodah days,
they assault & batter random negroes. They lynch.
On a roll, the rabble raze & burn the belongings
belonging to sympathizers & abolitionist
Republicans.

EYE OF THE BLACK VOICE:
Arise the matter of the Civil War, the war of
brother against brother, North against South, the war
of Emancipation, the war between the states.

VOICE OF THE BLACK EYE:
History records the Union prevails, not due
to ideology or being on God's side,
but to the evolution of Industry: pulleys
& levers & steam; a no-unions factory system
mass producing steel, munitions, processed food &
off-the-rack wear. Period.

EYE OF THE BLACK VOICE:
See the **1870**s,
where we started, way back. See
smokestacks' emissions
belching into the Northern sky
as from Moloch after a meal.

RASTUS:
Meanwhile, see the South. See
the South still waaaayyy
behind after getting
its agrarian, slave dependent booty
taken to the woodshed & the rod
not having been spared.

VOICE OF THE BLACK EYE:
See the smoke like snakes
of repudiation
> go up
>> as the
smoke of a furnace.

War, Sherman
(William Tecumseh,
1820–1891, former
San Francisco banker)
shows, is
sho nuff
> Hell.

RASTUS:
See tough battling Billy Sherman speak gruffly
of his red neck rivals.

SHERMAN:
*"If the people of Georgia raise a howl against
my barbarity and cruelty, I will answer
that war is war, and not popularity-seeking."*

RASTUS:
See
Sherman, the A-Merican Master
Of the Game of War
March
to the Sea. See
The South's magnolias
dragging in the dust.

PADDY:
But

wait.
Hear the up beat down beat
as they come to order, strike up the band, *ONE,*
2, *THREE,* 4.

RASTUS:
&
the rich get richer, the poor need more, *ONE,*
2, *THREE,* 4 &
Time & The Press & Church & State Forward March,
as the band plays on, & on with the show.

PADDY:
Hear the faint strains of Hope. Hear the faint tambourines
& riddles & fiddles & clacking bones of
MINSTRELSY sounding, like a last-reel bugle call,
& the thundering hoof beats of our charging
cavalry of blackened faced faux coon troupes.

RASTUS:
See their MINSTREL Cossacks turn the Dixie tide
by bolstering flagging Southern pride.

I. M. WELLBOURNE:
(Voice of the upper class)
See the Union North. Changed, but all the better for
the recent dust up.

PADDY:
See the Old Rich. The Better Sort. Cosmopolitan
Jamesian types, Henry (1843–1916), prim, repressed,
self-possessed, a part, proudly imperialistic
(the Rich who got Richer).

I. M. WELLBOURNE:

See the triumphant North's new consumers:
colorfully clad, but threadbare Bowery boys,
or b'hoys, & their breed, the new hooligan A-
MERICA, the rising ranks of the squat middle,
the post-war invention of the wage slaves of cogs,
sprockets, pulleys & levers, rails & steam, the
contented straddler class.

PADDY:

Peopled with those not content to be huddled. Inert.
Matter.

RASTUS:

The patched swarm, who itched to be treated white, while
still trapped in the amber of A-meric's point
of view, seeing it as the only standard of
measure.

I. M. WELLBOURNE:

While (Ha Ha) they prattled about their slaughterhouse
tastes in fuddled patois. They believe labor will
lift them from the pit of their station (nudge nudge)
a spade load at a time. Believe their brood will rise
up from the ditch.

RASTUS:

Believe they will be washed of their blemishes, faults
& stigmas in the anointing waters of
Capitalism. See them positioned by the
Kings of Commerce like thick doors latched against the still
lower mass.

I. M. WELLBOURNE:

See the North's entertainment notions further rent.

RASTUS:

See those who believe they will rise up & go their
own way, men of the city, in their glory turn
from High-Culture concert halls.

PADDY:

& European hoity-toity, see us cold
shoulder the salons of the bluenosed *bourgeoisie* &
collect in the dance halls & dives of New (post-war)
Democracy.

I. M. WELLBOURNE:

Wallowing in cheapside entertainment's polluting
dross & dregs as cocky as roaches.

RASTUS:

& itching for a scrape, they strut, thief thick, through the
slink & scurry of 5 Points, Chinatown &
Bowery Street's circus of brothels, music halls,
drug dens & shadowy saloons.

PADDY:

See the Most Favored launch home front assaults on the
threatened fief of Proper Diversions.

I. M. WELLBOURNE:

See us turn our backs on the bucking & cooning
Minstrel jiggery A-
merica.

RASTUS:

Down with dribble for slop jars!

I. M. WELLBOURNE:

Long live Old World chalice-worthy past-time potables!
consumed to commend the continuance of our
reign over those below the rank of Free White Persons.

P. T. BARNUM:
STEP RIGHT IN,
ALL WELCOME
1, 2, 3, 4
ON ON ON,
ON WITH THE SHOW!

PADDY:
But for the real bare knuckled, blue chipped, bust a gut, have
what it takes, rock 'em sock 'em, never say die, diehard, gilt edged,
keep smiling, worth its own weight in gold
amusement, no-thing succeeds like the successful
blackened faced MINSTRELSY, with the RED, WHITE & BLUE
all A-MERICAN blackened *Doodah!*
continuing to content after 3 decades,
& as simply as all A-MERICAN pie,

Coons
is buffoons.

EYE OF THE BLACK VOICE:
Hear the up beat down beat as they come to
order, strike up the band,
ONE, 2, THREE, 4,

VOICE OF THE BLACK EYE:
& the rich get richer, the poor need more,
ONE, 2, THREE, 4
& Time & The Press & Church &
State Forward March, as the band plays on, &
on with the show.

EYE OF THE BLACK VOICE:
1871
& unstoppable P. T. Barnum, late of the
A-merican Museum of New York, & his
humble beginnings with Joice Heth, grosses

4 hundred thousand \$ in the first season of
"The Greatest Show on Earth." 65 railroad cars
are required to transport his troupe. By 18-
74 they will humbug 20,000 folks
per day at 50 cents a head.

VOICE OF THE BLACK EYE & PADDY:
&
"Coons
is
buffoons."

RASTUS:
&
it is through their mutual attraction
to the message & diversions of donkey-simple
MINSTRELSY that Yankees & Confederates
fathom the commonality: after all *"they"* are,
each says of the other, Our A-MERICAN
Cousins! (Doodah.)

VOICE OF THE BLACK EYE:
That, therefore, is The Answer: the
common denominator, between these
directional & sectional antipodes,
the covenant enabling the healing of
the breaches thereof & the reforming of a more
perfect union.

RASTUS:
Hear A-MERICAN singing:
"Coons
is buffoons." (Hip hip!)

& *that* (Hurrah)
as simple as pie, as elementary as
gunning cod in a keg, chub in a tub, is

the long & short of it, the brass tacks, the bed rock,
the nub, the nut, the what's what, the substance & sum,
the water & crumb, the soul, the kernel, the core,
the scoop, the score, the crux, the gist & grist, the heart & guts,
the bolts & nuts, the nitty *&* the gritty:

PADDY:
*"Coons
Is buffoons."* Period.

EYE OF THE BLACK VOICE:
O,
My.

PADDY:
That
in a nut shell
is the Domestic Policy,
the rallying cry.

RASTUS:
That
cut & dry.

PADDY:
"Coons is buffoons."

EYE OF THE BLACK VOICE:
Sigh.

CHAPTER
9

 Reprise of the Bridge Crossing Theme

A Variation with a Blues Tinge

Exeunt.
 Flashback:

Bog. Chilling,
billowing caul of wet cotton like
Wolf Man-night-fog.
His hand
out
stretched,
fingering the gloom. Too clammy-thick
to detect friend from foe,
or who goes there? Toe, in this atmosphere,
hiding seeker & the sought;
inching like the tip of a blind man's cane.
Rastus. Runagate.
Way-quester in the unfit night of his middle passage,
divines a rise. It may be,
after mirror-imaged centuries of descent in the brumous vale,
the way up; or a dream; an angle of ascent,
or boundaries' limit; means of escape, or
metaphor. The greige grief of distressed lessons reaped
from the disenchanted plots of A-Merica
leapt to mind: expect nothing; expect anything.
A footbridge. Wooden span over darkness-surrounded water's

hidden changing face.

& what's that sound?
Not a howl or haint *Hoo.*
Not the feared chorus of unleashed hounds on the hunt;
noses to the ground in quavering harmony
with the melody of their prey's vibrating scent;
not the arrhythmic drumbeat of yelps & barks
announcing their findings to trailing masters with bated
huffs of rashed gray-breath, whose lanterns advance
like glowing,
cycloptic eyes.
No. A voice—
call in undertow—no—or is it?
—from ahead—behind—
—or under
ground? Or at all.

In acoustics 2 concurrent sounds =
simultaneous masking (nudge nudge),
(màs'kîng) noun,
as we already know, is the "concealment or
screening of one sensory process or sensation
by another." (Nudge again, 2 times.)
But these 2 sounds, sharing a frequency band
hum to him, come to him, a hankering forth
as 1, though not even as a sound,
but pressure waves pounding,
as resolute as heartbeats,
up through his soles,
& as a picture in the particled mist,
like memory through the murk, like the gauze through which
he moves. *"Style is the man himself,"*
it says. *"In nature there is nothing absolute,*
nothing perfectly regular," it says.

What it is, unbeknownst & of no concern to him, is the voice of

Georges-Louis Leclerc, Comte *de Buffon*. That's right. 1 mo' time
for emphasis. Comte de *Buffon*, nudge nudge. The near homophonic
coincidence

buffoon/Buffon
is almost too good to be true. The *Comte de Buffon*! COMTE—(kɔnt),
being a French title of rank, of which the English form is COUNT.
Leclerc (1707–1788).

A French naturalist with his *Histoire Naturelle, Générale et Particulière*,
whose approach allows him to see with a big eye: systems & patterns,
centrality & diversity, simplicity & complexity.

Like the immixture of history & time
in that neck of the woods at that moment.
"Never,"
it says, *"think that God's delays are God's denial,"*
it says.
Rastus, considering possibilities:
Might be a ghost, task undone, unfolding from its grave;
or dispatch from high heaven; or yet another
demon, disguised, tush, tush, to assail me—usurp
yet again; or a consoling drafts—
man of epigrams 'round which to rally; a Virgil,
illuming a path up-out & on 'way from this here
primeval purgatorial expanse of my
debunkers mocking ways. *"Hold on; hold fast; hold out,"*
it says. *"Patience is genius,"* it says. Yes, Rastus
knows, with patience a fly can eat an ox.

Buffon reasons beyond the accepted limits of his time. &, as a bonus,
he signifies on the manhood of A-merica's whites to boot. Doodah.

He says they are far less virile than their European counter parts,
he says, not qualifying or quantifying by class or creed. Indeed this
just might be a voice to hearken & cling unto like unto a raft in a
tidal wave of ridicule rocked by a storm of disdain. For upcoming

engagements with biology, zoology & comparative anatomy the *Comte de Buffon* sets theme, tempo.

Humming, in B-flat, the sound picture flashed forward
as a *"deviation from the local ambient
pressure . . . at a given location and given
instant in time."* It maps in Rastus
in an unimpeded dance of particles from
a vector some centuries ago: A Warrior. Left hand
in front of him; receptor, warning & counter-
balance, right cocked back, the spear alert as the tip
of a blind man's cane; charging uphill toward
a down-charging white haired, goateed, eagle eyed beast
in star-bannered top hat, index finger pointed.
It is of = parts malice, fraud, violence,
ambition & incontinence. It wants him.

What the voice is, unbeknownst & of no concern to Rastus, is,
on closer scrutiny Buffon, alas; could be a man of our time.
For he too had put in his mouth words against them that sought
abatement,
a place of refuge from the furor poured mightily down upon them as
they were hurled in the windy tempest of persecution, but finally they
received no relief,
no parting of the cloud, no cessation, no calm; saying of the native
African
that he had *"little intelligence"* but *"a great deal of feeling."*
Seems even for Buffon,
Doodah,
coloreds is coons & coons is buffoons.

It is that spirit that had se(n)t Rastus, covered
by darkness (nudge nudge) into flight & that sustains
him, the wait of A-merica on his back as he
clamors up a dew slicked slope, through wet web's umbra,
to higher ground, to again take aim at the star,
glowing like Frederick Douglass' eyes.

CHAPTER

10

 Reconstruction & Beyond

William T. Sherman, Eadweard Muybridge &

Syncopated Loco-Motion of Moving Images

& the Transcontinental Railroad

1871–1877

Fade forward to **1871**.

Hear the inspiriting Sousa like umph! umph!
umph! umph! See the Confederate colors,

> the Stars & Bars
> being
> run
> up
> the
> flag
> staff. All

is not lost. See the South in retrograde Re-
construction. See the North turn its back on landless, lobby-lacking
negroes, & see the sun setting on those reconceived darkies' false
hopes. See their for-
ward motion stopped in its tracks. Stopped? Or only
slowed
again,
like move-

ment in the 1870s photographs of
Eadweard James Muybridge (1830–1904)
a self-invented Englishman, née Edward James Muggeridge,
the father of the movies, acquitted murderer,
& A-MERICA's first rag-time photographer.

The pictures, so-called *sun drawings* of Muybridge,
moved. Riffled in rapid succession they
are a frieze of reconstructed notions of loco-motion &
time, often in silhouetted shades against stark
whiteness, or white starkness,
depending on the section you're seated in.
He slowed time.
Showed time
slowed.
Syn·co
pat·ed it to a flicker so the common man might
glimpse the complexities of visual prosody,
the scansion of tem·po, me·ter, the graphic re-
presentation of ca-dence with a hitch & a
halt, you know, a *"Wheel about*

> *& turn about, do*
> *just so . . ."*

like in the gait of
Jim Rice's apocryphal *"Negro character*
on Southern plantations."
E. Muybridge's renowned stop-time
series on Occident prove a trotting horse does,

as Negroes often must, move forward without their
feet touching the ground.

Quick dissolve back to 1863–1869.
Add (a) nitroglycerin,
(b) The Most Magnificent Project Ever Conceived,
(c) Orientals & work gangs of the common
slew of suspects & rejects into the mix, then
stay tuned for yet another inspiring & wretched
tale of A-MERICAN can-do.
On the soundtrack: the trance inducing 4/4
of tom toms & chug chug chug chug of wheels on steel
& ballads & reels of backcountry Anglo Celtics
& the form-seeking call & response moans of the
"emancipated" & the cosmological
5 tone inflected affects of Chinese music
& the triple time bobs & jerks of Irish jigs.
Music of the world of the workers, carried-over
from whence now aids & eases their cross
country cross-over of their daily lift & tote,
lift & tote.

Long shot:
        Wide-ranging turmoil. See separate but
linked struggles as East meets West & North meets South.
See the invaders in each instance benefiting
from the tried & true subjugators' tactic of
consolidation through destruction, y'know,

multiplication through subtraction, employed
against an entrenched way of life, in the name
of unification & progress toward a
continent united under the eagle's wing-
span. & in the doing opening the way
for the right of entry of Speculation,
Opportunity, Settlement, Religion &/
or the A-MERICAN drive to escape to (some-
one else's) territory, indigenous folk,
to be specific. Of whom Sherman, Union
terrorist bad ass, remember, who, recently
in the North/South sector, signified to his
Southern opposition, *"The North can make a steam
engine, locomotive, or railway car; hardly
a yard of cloth or pair of shoes can you make."*
Then in a demoralizing display of macho
militarism humbled the rebels,

          but changed
his tune when it was time for the piper to be
paid, by cutting them mucho slack.

Note: Sherman was a loud & avowed & unapologetic white
supremacist. Nigger was his name for those he reluctantly elevated
from the disenfranchised to wage slaves.
Note: Sherman signed an armistice that re-stored to the South
the very slaves & privileges they thought they'd lost forever: The
gentle-man's agreement not only did not guarantee the emancipation
of slaves, but affirmed prewar Southern property rights & state
governments & granted carte blanche amnesty. Doodah.
Note: Sherman did sign much discussed 40 acres & a mule
SPECIAL FIELD ORDERS, No. 15, granting land on off-coast
islands & *"abandoned rice-fields . . . 30 miles back from the sea."*
Note: It came to naught as President Andrew Johnson,
knuckling under to good old boy pressure, nixed it. Johnson (1808–
1875), segregationist successor to Abe Lincoln, assassinated while at
the theater. Doodah.
Hear the lamentations of the lobby lackers continue to take shape.

Sherman, rewarded for his deeds, succeeds U. S. Grant as
commander in chief of the U.S. Army.

But for now, in our flashback time frame, the Great Plains
is held by Sioux, Cheyenne, Arapahoe & Kiowa.
Separately & together they see no benefit
to a War Department backed railroad snaking through
their plains where the deer & the antelope & elk
& buffalo play.
            Sherman studies the state of
affairs, says, of the natural human
inhabitants, *"The more we can kill this year, the less
will have to be killed the next war, for the more I see
of these Indians, the more convinced I am that
they will all have to be killed or be maintained as
a species of paupers."* Having the troops to back
him up the big wheels keep on rolling, upgrading
from overland trails to an iron road of
overland rails, *"To carry the heavy load,"* to quote
"The hardest working man in show business," James Brown,
(A-merican singer, "Godfather of Soul"
[1933–2006]), through
the dissolving of the Continental Divide
via the building of the Transcontinental
Railroad (That Most Magnificent Project Ever
Conceived). It is a task of titanic under-
taking (nudge nudge) told in the toil of 90%
Chinese manpower, who happen to be between
jobs due to being barred by biased laws from
prospecting gold. Cussed as coolies, chinks, considered
too small too short to spike & drill & blast through
granite mountains & span ravines & salt flats,
prairie & desert, & pick & spade & haul &
lay & level miles of ties & rails, but recruited
finally as labor of last resort (because
the 1st choice good white men were surrendering to
gold & silver's siren songs).

While from the east
working west, a repertory of engineers,
surveyors, cooks, mechanics, hewers, haulers;
immigrants, mostly Irish, Mormons (young men
going west), vets of the late Blue & Gray, & the
recently partially enfranchised.

Hear, in stereo, left channel & right, the work
being done along the trail way: scuffling, shuffling
of buxie & boots; 13-foot rails blunt-thumping
onto the ties, clanged quavers when banged end to end,
lick setters metronomic refrain & *humph!* &
grunt & ring of sledge strikes, 3 to a spike, 10 spikes
to a rail, 400 rails to a mile, & the
clamor & tangle of accents & tongues, thunder
of hoof beats & gun shots in the distance, thud of
downed buffalo, hunter's hoops, hollers, &/but
there is, under the sweat & stink, no harmony,
no resonant accord, no melody of off
hours amity not in the scent of ethic
edibles, not in the buzzard fattening
buffalo carrion killed for sport & left to
rot. Young Bill Cody, maestro marksman, conducts
the A-mericanist counterpoint of slaughter
to the ecological symphony of Plains
Indian life. Kills a minimum of 12 per
day for the meat eating pleasure of the westward
destined workmen laying waste to the way of life
of the Sioux, Cheyenne, Arapahoe & Kiowa.

Whether by cosmic design, dumb luck, or some
mathematical equation of mayhem,
the duplicating of Sherman's Southern strategy
brought like results 'mongst the natives. The destruction
of forage & food effectively finished
the Plains people's ability & will to fight.
"Once built & in full operation," Sherman says

of the railroad, *"the fate of the buffalo &*
Indian was settled for all time to come . . . now
the wild game is gone, the whites too numerous and
powerful; . . . the Indian question has become
one of sentiment and charity, but not of
war."
Good old A-MERICAN know how. DOODAH, DOO
DAH DA.

      DashDotDot DashDashDash DashDot Dot.
Done.
Accomplished. Fini. The upgrading from overland
trails to an iron road of overland rails.

When the final coffin nail like spike strike rang,
& the twains, East & West, coupled at Utah's
Promontory Summit, the expulsed were swept in
the clickaty ticking clackity tocking *loco-*
motion onrush of the future, flipping like
Muybridge flash cards, till who they were & all they'd been
nearly vanished in the accelerating blur
before their own eyes, as the ocean to ocean
passage shrank from 4 months to 1 week & whites swarmed
like locusts & did cover the face of the divide,
& did consume & did smite. Yes, Sherman, wrong as he
was, was right

☛ Note: Upon retirement, Sherman, who had a reputation as a
fancy step dancer, danced midnights away at cotillions & balls. He
also attended theatre & was a colorful public speaker. Doodah.

CHAPTER

11

 Jim Crow Crosses Over from

Entertainment to Law,

the Parallel Rise of Klan-Whiteface in White Face,

& Black Faced Blackface & Slave Spirituals

Cross cut:
(after a quick glance back to 18-
68 & the black codes & Jim Crow laws
Making a mockery of the 14th Amendment's
protection of property rights for the freed slaves)
see 1877.

Slow pan down to Dixie.

RASTUS:
(Voice over)
See the last Federal troops, Doodah, marching home.
Hurrah, hurrah. See Home Rule, a.k.a. State's

Rights, right? restored, & see The South reinvented.
See the Ku Klux Klan, that noxious blossom of the

bitter fruit nurtured in bloodied soil & reaped
from the weedy vineyard of defeat . . . What evil lurks . . .?
The shadowy Klansman knows. See defenders of
white, Protestant, Christian A-merica rise. Ride. Clippityclopp.
See costumed terrorists, their
white faces in white face, disguised as the ghosts
of the Confederate dead, intending that coons,
carpetbaggers & their kind shall be horribly
afraid of thee & shall bow themselves down &
tremble & be troubled in thy presence & shall
quake at thy word & *"theatrical flair"* & be
kept in our place. &, oh yes, there *is* popular
agreement to the end of their means, though some
quiet quibbling over their methodology.

Pan back a moment, see the bigger picture. See
The South, as Northern money sees it (after having
seen to it), see it ripening for raw
Industrialization. Cheap labor, artisan
& otherwise, roving the streets like Bo Peepless
sheep. *"Give 'em another decade, see how they sort
themselves out. Then we'll make our move,"* Big Money says.
See the South being redeemed, resurrected
in its own Currier & Ives image.

       See the molten
impressions of the disenfranchised, being cast
in the South's new fiery foundries of affliction.

          See
a mess of new golliwogs. A complete line of
buffoon coons: mammies, a'nties, uncles, boys &
assorted spooks, sambos & pickaninnies,
mass produced for the psychic knickknack and notion
shelves of the new common Men A-MERICAN con-
sumers. See
    an industry of degradation
lift every voice & twang: *"Coons is buffoons."* See

the South's old regime bobbing like life buoys on
the sea of tranquility. See it rising like
whitecaps cresting on a wave of legislative
activity. See a confederacy of
Black Codes being enacted.

                          Twill by'n'by, Lawd
'a' mussy, see the New Confederacy turn
the tide against the shadowy skies of change. See
the return of the Promised Land of Tradition
& its conditions & Glamour of the Good Old Days.
See the leopard retain his spots. See the wolf re-
gain his voice. See the Good Ol' Boys, the Southern
Democrats, rule. See these postulates of exclusion
take physical shape, be nailed to the door, rata-
tattat, like Martin Luther's theses.

                WHITES
                ONLY.

See the capital-less spoils of war, the seventh
sons, the buffoon coons, the traditional fodder,
fertilizer & fuel of Dixie doings, being
nailed in their place. Rat-atatatattatat. See that
positioning being de rigueur for the psychic
& commercial health of the Dear Old Southland. Rat-atattat.
See the dark cloud of equity
departing. Rat-atat. See the Confederate
flag a-flapping in the bright blue. See the final
chapter close, ratatattat, ratatattat, rat-
atattatratatattat, on that Unspeakable
Tragedy. See The South restored, Lawd a mussy.

& the land has rest from war, *ONE*, 2, *THREE*, 4. &
it is the best of times, Glory Halle-lujah.
But
wait.

What,

you ask,
what about the antebellum &
post-war troupes of all-colored *comiques*?
The upstaged
& unsung companies of *"coal black brothers"* &
"sooty sisters" whose musical, vocal &
dancing acts blossom like heliotropic blooms
seeking the sun of recognition in the dark
night of A-MERICA?

What of them?
No longer Massa & Missy's pride & prized
hybrids doing double duty—being bearer
of the burden of the before the hyphen title
would seem enough—but having to be
holding *plus* diversion: footman-fiddler; field-hand-
banjo picker, seamstress-soprano; pickaninny-
playmate-dancer—meant a double yolk on them, &
we're ever on call; summoned to socials & balls
& put through our *"art-less"* but enthralling stunts &
paces. Providing off-hours entertainment
for their guest's pleasure, self-validation & un-
responsive pity to their plaintive selections.
No longer only that. Or are we? . . .

Lo & alas, Gentle Reader, note the prospect
of that fool's goal—entrance into Show Business's
"cultural industry"
via descent into
the heart of that dark matter in search of the form
for a light, blackened blackfaced cash on the barrelhead
entertainment: notion affirming pleasure
during the All A-MERICAN huddled muddle's
leisure—the alchemical transmutation from
fact to artifact, from plantation parlor
amusement to paid professionals.

KID MALONE:

(Prototype colored blackened faced Minstrel)
We "Ethiopian delineators" are,
at this late hour, let up, to get up in black-
ened face & Minstrel get up & get up on the
(Hah Hah) *"legitimate stage"* & carry on in
the (so-called) All "A-MERICAN musical
entertainment tradition," on the condition
we too (as our burnt-cork faced white *"betters"* do)

romp

& spin while grinning the mindless but *"winning"* grin-
&-bearing-it-grin though resenting, lamenting
being restricted to presenting, without
obviously augmenting either of MINSTRELSY's
2 traditional faces: 1: the cowed & "well
cared for" rustic darkie, lustless & contented
in our idyllic indigence. Or, 2: the laughing-
stock, fish-out-of-water, Northern negro dandy,
captured in all our inglorious comic in-
eptitude. (Hah Hah), for Minstrelsy, *"The only
original A-MERICAN institution"*
(as slavery should have been billed before it, doo dah),
true, unmitigated, red white & blue dyed
in the wool, Mainstream Minstrelsy, in formula,
form & philosophy is what it is, what it
had been & what it has to be if it is to
be what it is intended to be: a line of
racial & cultural demarcation, demon-
strating to All A-MERICAN audiences,
who ha-ha'ed first, without questioning after, their
laughter. So, still, at this late hour, we new black
entertainers, long exiled to the impoverished
fields of our enforced apprenticeship; & on whose
foundation the House of Minstrelsy is built &
whose songs are sung as hymns & HawHawHaws to our
kith, kin & cultures' inferiority &
insolence;

enter, getting the bum's-rush in where
disguised men sneered for bread;

                                enter, with no hounds
in behind—escape by virtue of rote routine,
a step at a time out of the "back break" business,
& onto the stage. With less concern for the
politics or politic & more for the wage,
the loot, the booty, the *"In God We Trust"*;

                                        enter,
maligned, undermined, red lined—as we had known we
would be—;

                  enter, expecting vexation with-out
representation or equal compensation;
enter, mere fretting foils reaping only spoils, but
with eyes wide open after shadow-shuffling
for a couple centuries through the valley of
dearth;

                enter the Business, capering & cutting
buckles in the blank face of other's original
sin (knowing which restrictions applied, but enter
with hope, knowing hope is a process, not a blinding
bromide, knowing first hand, that with stereotypes
it ain't only what's in them, but equally &
ironically the veiled bits & whits left out that
sting, smart & throb the deepest);

                                  enter, to be
IGNORAMUSES AMUSEUS, the new fools, the
dancing, singing lackeys lacking socially re-
deeming worth save as fresh twists on old themes;

                                        enter

& *"Find out,"*
as the song says,
     "what they want
       and how they want it, and
       give it to them
       just that way." (Hah Hah)

                        —just

adopting maneuvers to adapt; adapting
maneuvers to adopt: *"Deceive and eat,"* play the
fool for pay, land on their feet. So who,
to be true, is the bumpkin, the dullard, the dummkopf,
the dunce? The cluck, the schmuck, who the schlemiel, for real?
Who the fool? The user? Who the tool? Is a fool
a fool if he's (a) fooling fools who want, will pay,
perhaps need to be fooled? or (b) only if he's
enough of a fool to fool around and show he
knows who is truly the fool, or (c) worse, if he
truly is a fool, and is such a fool he is
too foolish to even see it? So, for the
arising blackened faced black Minstrels—to be or
not to be that false, but wildly popular rendering
of ourselves, is hardly a question. It is the
business of the Business.
                    "God's delays are not God's
denials."
          The market demands it, & it is
a consumer's market.
                    Enter, not this time as
black sheep to our slaughter, but as Brer's Rabbit in-
to the briar patch. (Like 2 score & 4 bunnies
to Australia—remember?) This time we enter
as perpetuators & perpetrators.
(Remember too, be ever mindful of our double
dilemma, we dark strutters finally at the ball,
& of our need for our own sense of dignity
& mind's peace at our having to distance our selves
from our bogus show-time selves while managing, with
magical artistry to present the same gestures,
lines & pretense-depictions as our dispossessing
white predecessors, while, at one & the same time, (A)
confirm our supposed foolishness in the eyes of
our beholders & (B) (partially, at least) save face
by playing the hack-work bliss at one & the
same time, with the ever-nagging question, Does the

rendering of that humbling & demeaning,
but comforting to A-MERICA image give
aid & comfort which outweighs the benefits we
blackened faced blacks derive from it? So, with no more
sustaining us than our hope, our faith & belief
in our ability, proven by years of ex-
ploiting Job's message, chapter 21, verse 3,
*"Suffer me, that I may speak, and after that I
have spoken, mock on,"* i.e., of deceiving to eat;
so, enter, to play the fool, but affirm our selves;
enter the possibility of A-MERICA,
not, as with latter day immigrants, through the
"Golden Door" with the chance of becoming FREE WHITE
PERSONS & all that entailed, but from the wings, on-
to a shingled shore, hoping (simply?) to be seen
not so simply;

        enter, at least with less *"an oughts
an ought,"* the way they figure, *"all for the white man,
none for the nigger."* & for sure no more *"In the
fields 'fore day"* & *"Pick a bail of cotton."* No more
overseer's prod, roughshod & goad. Black Face black
Minstrelsy is a chance, a meal, a room,
the open road.

        But, prolongation of the true coon
convention & knowing our place, in the face
of it all, is as forlorn as a foregone
conclusion can be. It is as evident as
the sooted noses on our smutted faces.

              For,

as entertainingly authentic &
authentically entertaining as we were,
it remained the case, at the local level, we
crafty coons, for all our shrewdness, made scant progress
on matters of race. We still had to vacate all
white places, as warned by city limits signs,
before the color of the night matched the color
of our faces.

But, however tough it was, That's
Entertainment, we thought, & it was a damn sight
better than our previous line of work.
Doodah.

& as for our black faced audiences, you ask? What
must they have thought? Better, we must assume, they pre-
sumed, to see them-selves be their foolish selves, full
of high jinks & jubilation, ever ready
to break out in a shuffle or a song, each of
which were thought to be *au naturel* naturally
in their Negroid blood, than to be totally dis-
missed, not seen at all. Just about then, & on the
other hand, in an attempt to put another
face on it & try alternative marketing:
The Fisk Jubilee Singers, schooled songsters, singing
Slave spirituals, so-called, & rejoicing airs,
concertize less rude & crude tunes (& are therefore
"exceptions" to the Rule. But are billed, still, though, as
a novelty act). On an evening in 18-
82 in the White House, built by slave labor,
they harmonize on *"Safe in the Arms of Jesus."*
Chester A. Arthur (1829–1886),
the 21st President of the United
States, listens. Cries like a baby. The previous
evening the Jubilee singers had been refused
rooms in every hotel, tavern & inn in A-
MERICA's capital.
                    Doodah.

& from the black face beneath the black face, the side-
mouth *sotto voce* battle hymn:
Thine lies have been the story
through the cunning of mask and word;
            trampling, jigging and stamping about
            while we have gone unheard,
            but we will continue marching on.

CHORUS:
Huzza & hallelujah! Huzza &
hallelujah! Huzza & hallelujah! We
continue marching on. To stride where no true black
has tread a way is all we've ever sought to see
our truth portrayed our way, there's a right smart battle to
be fought. — CHORUS

The All A-MERICAN audience, who think they
see, but do not hear, laugh & laugh & laugh . . .

CHAPTER

12

W. E. B. Du Bois &

Booker T. Washington

Step Up & Step Out &

Black Minstrelsy Turns a Corner,

P. T. Barnum Crosses a Bridge, Rag Kicks Up Its Heels &

Thomas Jefferson Shows His Dark Side

1880s–1890s

———•◆•———

Mean-
while,
see William Edward Burghardt (W. E. B.)
Du Bois, Harvard's first colored Ph.D. & Fisk
& University of Berlin grad (born in
1868, the year the 14th Amendment
bequeaths paper citizenship on the once en-
slaved). See Du Bois, researcher, thinker, march to a
radical drummer. Hear Du Bois speak on the race
Problem from the ivied towers of academe.
Hear Du Bois i.d. Ignorance as race Problems'

chief cause. Hear him declare Knowledge & Culture the
Cure.
Mean-

while,
see Washington, Booker T. (1856–
1915), founder & first principal of
Tuskegee Institute, shake his head. Washington,
with the endorsement of Big White Money, urges
coloreds to take low, go slow, *earn* acceptance by
the sweat of their brow, but later, not now, as the
rich get richer, the poor need more, *ONE*, 2, 3, 4,
& Time & the Press & Church & State & the A-
MERICAN populace consumers, the A-
mericanists, Forward March as the band umph! umph!
umph! umph! plays on.

But behold then *umph! umph!* the new blackened
faced black black minstrels, in the tradition old as
underdogs—through charm, nimble capering
stake their claim as *"the original Negroes."* See
the black black minstrels, through subtleties, shadings &
the showing off of *"the real stuff"* (Hah Hah) out-con
the 2 faced faux-faced white coons, therefore & thereby,
as the *"genuine article"* begin to reveal
the real, replace the comic face, refine & re-
define the art, the craft, the warp & weft of
coonery. See coonery's grin slowly slacken.
See the soul beneath the surface slowly blacken,
while revealing the true glee *&* gloom at their core.
& see, Dear & Gentle Reader, it come to pass,
that, in the Eden of general conviction,

doubts regarding negroes pop up like sprout-tops
of crab grass, puncture weed or night shade. But, given
the clinging strength of traditional; endurance of
blind faith; tenacity of habit & the cocoon-
comfort of gullibility, the changing of
America's common men's minds slubs at a snail's
pace toward narrowing the divide 'tween
the party line & the order of the day; 'tween
a white lie & colored truth; 'twixt popular
amusements & civic matters

> (if, indeed, such a divide

e'er existed).
See, as further evidence, the turning of days
& leaves, till it is 1883. See Barnum.
Yes, him again ('twas a Barnum & Bailey world
after all). This go 'round he's paid public funds to
"sell" the Brooklyn Bridge, that is to prove to a
public doubtful of the strength & stability
of the new *"river span."* With
Jumbo, "The Towering Monarch of His Mighty Race,
Whose Like the World Will Never See Again,"
at his heels, said Barnum, master of bunkum, leads
a 21 pachyderm parade across the
"8th Wonder of the World." The public, convinced by
the stunt, follows, & the line (if, indeed it e'er
existed) thins yet again 'tween civic need,
municipal policy & popular Entertainment.

The foundations for said bridge, symbol of late 19th-century
innovation & progress, were laid 'neath the river by burrowing,
union-barred, little fish immigrants, in surreal pneumatic air-tight
casket-like cylinders that caused their pulses to rise & fall, slow &
speed, tick to a rag-time tock for 2 & a quarter bucks a day. Blasts,
fires & *"Caisson's disease"* (the bends) claimed more than 2 score of
A-MERICA's huddled, hapless muscle minions.

See **1886**. See the publication

of the 1st acknowledged Rag. *"All Coons Look Alike*
To Me," performed by a white man in black face. Penned
by Ernest Hogan, negro, yes, *"the unbleached A-*
merican," née, Reuben Crowdus, yes, blackened faced
black Minstrel & vaudevillian. It's a tongue in
cheek, clear eyed critique on a cockeyed concept. *"To,"*
as Countee Cullen (1903–1946)
perplexed, *"make a poet black, and bid him sing!"* as
if that were an enigmatic thing.

Thomas Jefferson, in all his pragmatic
intelligence & cocksure signifying, said,
if not first, at least earlier, *"Misery is*
often the parent of the most affecting touches
in poetry. Among the blacks is misery
enough, God knows, but no poetry." (Ouch.)
Thom (1743–1826),
who said, *"He who permits himself to tell a lie*
once, finds it much easier to do it a second
and third time, till at length it becomes habitual,"
is called out by his contemptuous
contemporaries as the Negro President,
not like up-coming Warren G. Harding;

thought to have
negro blood bubbling like brown sugar through his veins,
but because the Southern gentlemen enslavers,
controlling their black bloc of 3/5s vote per slave,
casting the majority for T.J. putting
him over the top, as it were, shooing him in,
in 1800, president #3
of the new nation, *"conceived in liberty &*

*dedicated . . . "*you know, *". . . where all men were created*
=." Note the ironic hypocrisy, or
hypocritical irony. Jefferson:
astronomer, surveyor, surgeon, architect,
lawyer, vet, musician, inventor, congressman,
political philosopher, University
of Virginia founder, governor, minister
to France, secretary of state, vice-pres & drafter
of the Declaration of Independence, based
on the theory of natural rights, detailed in
its enumeration of specific grievances
& injustices, concluded, regarding blacks, *"Love*
is the peculiar oestrum of the poet.
Their love is ardent, but it kindles the senses
only, not the imagination." Oestrum, he said,
"the peculiar oestrum." What bottle of flies have
you uncorked here, Thom? Oestrum having to do with
the period during which female mammals are
in heat; capable of conceiving. Why'd Goochland,
V-A born, Thomas, who swore, *"eternal*
hostility against every form of tyranny
over the mind of man," go to oestrum, do you
think? Why, sans hawing or hemmings, did that sally
forth? Do you think it had as much to do with
the definer as the defined, who said himself
(of himself?), *"Resort is had to ridicule*
only when reason is against us." It was
a rearing, as with Hamlet's daddy's ghost, of some
dark heat, some pent up nostrum in the prison house
of Thom's own psyche, revealing more tangled &
cordoned plenum in his private politics than
dreamt of in his public philosophy; that perhaps
rendered to him the notion of black creativity
insuperable, not to say indecipherable;
that the techniques of blackened faced Black Face,
as enslaved sorcery & bewitchment before it,
was transposing irony & doubling

2-faced entendres, spitting out its spite through
another's mouth as the intemperance of clouded
minds & mutterings. Jefferson, at his death
on the 4th of July, uttered, *"Nunc Dimittis,
Domine — Nunc Dimittis, Domine." "At last,
all-powerful Master,"* 2 times. He died Master
of *"130 Valuable Negroes."*
History does not note if they sang.

*"None but a poet can write a tragedy. For
tragedy is nothing less than pain transmuted
into exaltation by the alchemy
of poetry,"* understood Edith Hamilton,
translator, classical scholar (1867–
1963).

"Find out," as Hogan's song says,
*"what they want
and how they want it,
and give it to them
just that way."* (Hah Hah)

See the unforeseen slowly dawn, like post-storm sun.
See, Gentle Reader, Minstrelsy's m.o. &
s.o.p. shy, sway & pale in the face of
the tide of blackened faced black contra-minstrelsy
& not just on-stage entertainers, but
managers, promoters, entrepreneurs;
organizing, promoting, owning their own shows —
like harvesters who'd formerly gathered only
niggardly reapings of the bitter fruit of slight
& oversight sown as seeds on stony places,
thorny waysides, & fallow fields 'cross barren land-
scapes of A-MERICA's insatiable need for
replenished notions on *"nat'ral"* ways of blacks, their
make up, their plain & picturesque fiddle faddle;
the tittle-tattle of their gibberish patter

& prattle & their deficits of mind, money
& morals —

        as, paradoxically, in the nation
that nurtured the notion of the coon, by the '90s
see Negro Minstrel shows blossom into big time:
full orchestras, daz'ling costumes, striking sets. The works.
'Tended by ebony belles & dark-town swells,
in hope that within the fraudulent form, flawed beyond
salvation, still some dignity could be found, &
that facet aired, declared. & yes, there, it turned out,
were darkskinned men who on the theory that
"it took a thief" . . . & *"fighting fire with"* . . . , they,
in their guise as half man half bullshit, proved apt
at negotiating the rigors of Minstrelsy's
maze by following the thread of hope, to escape
to the spotlight, with at least the half man intact.
"Holy Shit!" Coons wit' wit — a sign of progress,
given the prior appraisal of their status.
Philosophical & social & cultural questions
were also loosed from the dungeon's depths. Might old-minded
A-MERICAN blackened faced white Minstrelsy merely
be xenophobic balder-dash? Partisan
poppycock? Jingoistic bull? & of un-sound
fury signifying little or nothing? With-
out truth but deep consequences. See,
Kind & Patient Reader (an inside aside),
blackened faced black Minstrels don't, by any means, all
bolt from convention. Much remains the down-market
usual, the same old run of the mill bill, but
some of the new do, hot & proper, set the stage
& serve up the goods for what's to follow. So,
a question is, by bringing light to the black face
of night, while all but barring coloreds from the
conception & forum of the real &
metaphorical City dubbed *"White,"* was Progress
conspiring again' or for 'em?

CHAPTER

13

 Entering the White City

Shunted to the Shadowy Margins, but

Tapping Out a Syncopated Meter, a

New Tune, Whose Force Changed the

Way the White City Denizens Go About

Their Goings About & the Freedom &

Dignity with Which They Go About It

& the Relative Positions They Assume

in the New World A-Comin', Guest

Starring Christopher Columbus, Eadweard

Muybridge, Frederick Douglass, Ida B.

Wells, Little Eva, Frank Baum & Others

1893

See 18 hundred 93.
See all is fair —
the World's Columbian Exposition, a.k.a.
the Chicago World's Fair, a.k.a. (nudge nudge) *"The"*

(drum roll, please) *"White City,"*
"the most Significant and Grandest Spectacle of Modern Times"
where nights are electric
light bright, & the buildings shine blindingly white, yet,
blacks, backed, yet again, into the shadows, are barred
from contributing, except as consumers, or,
of course, as amusements.

The World's Congress Auxiliary

OF THE WORLD'S COLUMBIAN EXPOSITION

DEPARTMENT OF SCIENCE AND PHILOSOPHY

GENERAL DIVISION OF AFRICAN ETHNOLOGY

"NOT THINGS, BUT MEN"

See O'Kelly, *e pluribus unum,*
on line. Orderly. In step with the populace
with the price of admission. Inching toward the
entrance to the New World. The Future. He reads,
over the shoulder of an ironed, starched, and whisk broomed
hog butcher. The *Daily Tribune*'s rendering
of the 3 days past.
"The veil of mist was lifted from over the
White City."
Umph! *Umph!* to the military artilleries'
Boom! Boom! *Boom!* the Calvary's ClippityClop
ClippityClop & A-MERICA's brand new Pledge
of Allegiance to the 45 starred flag, &

the 5 thousand voiced chorus declaiming, *Umph! Umph!*
the *"Columbian March,"* Umph! *Umph!* followed by a
prayer, the Hallelujah Chorus from the *"Messiah,"*
Umph! *Umph!* the *"Star Spangled Banner,"* Hurrah! *Hurrah!*
more prayer, more Boom! *Boom* & nearing conclusion an
address by Stephen Grover Cleveland (18-

37–1908), 22nd & 24th
U.S. presidents. Cleveland, a Democrat,
"a fresh face" & a Presbyterian preacher's
boy, formerly a teacher in an institute
for the blind & later to write in the Ladies'
Home Journal, *"Sensible and responsible women
do not want to vote. The relative positions
to be assumed by men and women in the working
out of our civilization were assigned long
ago by a higher intelligence than ours."* Whose,
he didn't say, but he'd also previously
said, *"The United States is not a nation to
which peace is a necessity."* He says in his
Columbian Exposition opening remarks:
*"Let us hold fast to the meaning which underlies
this ceremony. . . . Let our hopes and aspirations
awaken forces which in all time to come shall
influence the welfare, the dignity & the
freedom of mankind."*
See.
See all of this, the Umph!
Umph!! Hurrah! & BoomBoom! take place 400 years
to the month after Christopher Columbus, re-
member him (?), a.k.a. Cristobal Colony,

a.k.a. Cristoforo Colombo, a.k.a.,
by royal proclamation, *"The Admiral,"* a.k.a.
(by self-proclamation) *"Ambassador
of God"* & Christo Ferens (Bearer of Christ) lurched
lost on to the New World, *"The Indies,"* as he called
it, the New World's Columbian Exposition,
a.k.a. *"The White City,"* opened in
                                        (to
parody 2nd City poet, Spanish-A-
merican war vet & fireman Carl Sandburg
[1878–1967])
sow slaying, wheat stacking, scrappy, gusty, broad
shouldered Chicago, Hurrah! Hurrah!
This, as
juvenescent A-merica was, by leaps &
bounds, outgrowing its agricultural roots as it
streamlined along the industrial track, Jack.
& so, the Expo seemed the right juncture to re-
consider itself, think about how it thought it ought
to be thought about, by itself & Others.
It thought it ought to be about time to strut its
stuff for all the world to see, respect & pay proper
homage to the engine of state fueling the *"progress
of civilization[s]"* hiss, chug, spark, arc, crank &
glow. So, the Fair's missions were to promote Pride &
Patriotism; turn a new face to the world
(& make a buck in the bargain) through its sundry
Fairway concessions & exhibits, premiering,
or helping to popularize Cracker Jacks, Pabst
beer, Cream of Wheat, picture postcards, hamburgers,
carbonated soft drinks, Aunt Jemima Pancake mix—
"Let the taste tempt you"—
the telephone, the phonograph, Juicy Fruit gum,
a moving sidewalk; map of the U.S. comprised
of pickles, a bridge of Kirk's soap, Statue of
Liberty from a block of salt, the Liberty Bell
replicated in California oranges,

"exotic" dancers, a village of rumored flesh
feasters straight out of Dahomey, a kitchen, all
electric, a 2 thousand ton Ferris Wheel
20 stories tall with 36 train car sized
wooden boxes, capacity 60 per,
rotated the fool hardy, O'Kelly in their
number, through 2 revolutions, 50 cent a head.

Barrel-head dollars bought admission to or
possession of each of the above, swelling the chests
of sponsors & allied marketeers, including
ticket fares from the continuous, but un-
synchronized procession of sun to sun choo-choos
chug-chugging from all points & independent lines,
into the depot of the City on the Prairie.
Each arrival & departure determined by
their local pastoral methods, the nature
of Nature back home; the way the world wheeled 'round &
'round the sun; modes of yore deemed no longer
tolerable in the rapidly Time & Distance
shrinking scheme of things technological. Of
necessity, a standardized chronometry,
regulating railway transport was, to avoid time-
wasting jams & wrecks, wired station to station,
coast to coast. Officially systematizing
& in the process, for good, or better, or worse,
changing forever the idea of Time & A-
MERICAN's alliance with & allegiance to it,
e.g., each morn's daybreak hour, moving east to
west, began & began & began, click & click
& tock & tick, like the frames of Muybridge's photos
in a flip-frieze of repeated, disjointed times,
dictated by the cadence of Commerce &
dedicated to clocking a nation hurtling
head-long t'ward the "World of Tomorrow"—the White City

Long shot: Stereoscopic aerial view from top of the Ferris Wheel:

the Midway Plaisance. Like a baker's board of Beaux Arts wedding
cakes a-shimmer in the sun.

MONTAGE: Administration Building. Agricultural Building. Court
of Honor. Grand Basin.

O'Kelly, Ryan: mechanic, at the zenith
of Ferris' contraptions' orbit. Scans the Fair:
Chicago, the lake, till it meets heaven. Wonders,
Is this, swaying in a gondola above groveling
rabble, the likes of the lot for uppity mucks
in their gilded cages? who, neither in the before
nor the over all 've ever toted their share,
yet dip deepest & most often from the pot.

Below. On the ground(s): Zoopraxographical Hall.
Eadweard Muybridge of (if your think-back needs a nudge
nudge) the moving still photographs, from back a decade or
2, lectures.

       Mister I. M. Wellbourne: of Money, armored
in the righteousness of certitude; confidence
of the uncontested, never once considering
consequence, pays to gaze at the zoopraxiscope
projections. & what to his wondering eyes do appear —
With hand-tremble, gut-tremor, exits.

                 & startled,
looks up at the sound of advancing hooves. Not
Muybridge's hurtling thoroughbred, but a team of
nags in tandem, hauling a wagon of empty
milk canisters back to the dairy barn. It passes,
rattling off-rhythms above the measured hoof beats,
its galvanized cargo, untethered, dances
akimbo about its splintered bed like Irish
drunks, or jigaboo dolls on jerking strings.

BOOTBLACK:
Shine? Captain Captain. Shine 'em so make your feet smile.

Shine from a shine, Wellbourne thinks without thought.
My boots *are* mud caked. Must've strayed in near daze
from the paved path. I'll sit. Re-collect myself
as the nap-headed, knickered little nigger whistles
& tends my shoes.

Staring, lightheaded, Wellbourne'd blinked. Before him
in the whitened brick Hall, projected, Muybridge's
lumbering menagerie of equines &
elephants had whizzed in forward march, a
Zoopraxiscopical Circus,
life-large.

The boy whistles some catchpenny, know-no-better
jig tune as his rag, lazy, almost tactile as
stroking a cat, hums accompaniment.

BOOTBLACK:
Be so black & shiny use'em for a mirror,
Captain Captain.

Wellbourne knew it'd been simulated; a simple
series of still images spun faster & faster.

Faster & faster the coon's rag sings &
snappity pop-Pop-Pops. Whirring like an upturned
bicycle wheel, its spinning invisible but
for the ancient song's gray murmur from the spokes.

WELLBOURNE:
But would *they*, the dull & ugly, understand? Would,
could their less reasoned minds not be addled,
as with their kind on the whiskey they swigged in their
bibulous intemperateness, & not be set
spinning? The pictures moved! they'd think, moved for heaven's sake!
At the speed of life! If the inanimate
moved they'd see no limits; think the laws of order

null & voided. Foundation stones might hurl heavenward,
& hail, without regard to station, or rank.

The sham-shimmying cloth a blur below the
tweeting titter-totter of the burr-head's hooey
& hiccupy tune.
                    A dark hum, half heard but
fully felt, like the warning of a heart beat skipped —
then — then — again.

I entered from an oak staunch world, but, upon
seeing the whirl of Muybridge's loco motion
it was as if I'd stepped into a revolving
door,
"always opened,
always closed"
(invented 1888)

& exited into a dizzying universe
of reeling unraveling (un)realities
flourishing & finding new & liberating
forms at this moment in the dawning of the morning
of A-merica's shining White City upon the Hill.

His boot bottom tapped tapped.

BOOTBLACK:
Thank you, Sir. I shined a skip in 'em,
so careful how you step now, Captain Captain."

WELLBOURNE:
(Fretting like a White City Chicken Little
fumbles, flips a coin at the riddle grin & moves
off, still unsteady, towards the Bazaar of Nations
on the Midway Pleasance.)
An omen of the unimaginable! They'll
think, "If pictures can move then longitudes &

latitudes of logic are scrambled! boundaries
& limits interloped! seasons shuffled from reason's
accustomed time. What was chronologic
is simultaneous." The Philistine multitudes,
like yoked beasts un-reined, out of step with disciplined
time will rush & push the pillars supporting
the roof of logic over the shining city,
& it will topple to shambles, somersaulting
like Ferris' cars rent from their rigging, or
Lucifer from Heaven, spin-hurtling down,

                              down,

                              down

                              through the

                              rabbit-hole

of Muybridge's jabberwocky world of movement.
This new notion of motion, this new senseless, dis-
jointed & tangled-tattered time corrupts the way
things are (are intended to be!); further corrodes
the divide between matters moving in leisured
& controllable patriotic flow of
manifest exclusion, Nationalistic Hope
& the threatened who-knew-what-all of this hurried,
herky-jerky beginning of the sorrows. Would
the underling flock of newly hatched & patented
common man Henny-Pennys & Goosey-Looseys,
after having their noggins stampeded by a
deluge of life as it might be: electricity,
telephones, phonographs . . . could they be led yet
again down the backward, counter-clockwise trail
to that garden of naked Edenic ignorance &
(un)natural belief in the righteousness of
fundamentalist unbalance? & be content with
the same ol' chicken feed of the consumption
of goods & Gilded, be-dangled, star spangled
jingoism? Or, worse, far worse, will the threadbare,
armed with their natural wiliness, hitched with the rousing
hope bespoke in the Fair's every hall & booth,

lead them, with unbound speed, from our lessons of the fixed
& favored, to plot new directions or objectives
against our benefit? Will the warp & weave of
law & order be tattered to rags?

BOOTBLACK:
(Watches Wellbourne, trying to get his bearings, slight
stutter in his step—like he's been nudged—[nudge nudge].)
What the dark matter with you now, Br'er Captain Captain,
you done wobbled off the beaten path of self-
fulfilling tracts, onto ground that shifts beneath your
dearest fancies. Another misstep, at the
intersection (or crossroads!) of Shadows & Smoke(s);
might, in a blink or wink, peep a flicker of the span,
the range of the coming siege of change. Change that'll
sound deeper than your old Foxy-Loxy, flag draped,
stiff, self-serving stance of standing pat. Be like being
shaken awake by a thudding, limb-jerk chest-thump
—to the nightmare of insight into the depth
of your blindness. Face it. Trust what you see. But, well,
ain't, lo those many years, ain't *"seeing is believing"*
been y'all's premise, point, foundation, bread & butter,
mother's milk nourishing the aim & imagery
of Minstrelsy? Best get a grip, Captain Captain,
going need you a sticking place against the suck
of the center of A-merica's teeny tiny
black hole swirl-whirling round faster & faster,
trying to consume all before it in a dog
eat dog (or, as with Br'er Little Black Sambo),
tiger by the tail blur, whose gravitational
field is so concentrated, intense, resolute
& dense, till no thing, not even the light of White
City's white, can escape being swallowed into
its own accelerated Fall, not with a whimper,
but a Big old skitty nitty gritty Bang! (Nudge
nudge.)

Heel tap. Then toe. *"What's that sound!?"*
Spooked (nudge nudge) Wellbourne jumps.
Wheels about . . .
turns about . . .

"Sounds like a long distance call," sings Muddy Waters
from Rolling Fork, Mississippi
(1915–1983), *"The Hoochie Coochie Man"*
who couldn't be satisfied. Sounds
like a long distance call from the center of the Dark
& the fringes of the Fair. A syncopated, high stepping March
of a brand new
Time.
Rag-
time
like a genie that poofed from the uncorked
vessel of colored saloons, pool halls
& sporting houses, to materialize onto the bright
lighted mid-way of the *"White City"* of A-merica's
dawning awareness.

      Wellbourne, meandered the *"Beaux*
Arts" promenades with the *"barbarous & the*
barely civilized" on display & in attendance
as the thumping rhythms of rags by Scott Joplin
& a phalanx of piano professors,
on the grounds & in environs near & far.

INSERT: *"Street in Cairo."* See *"strange sights."*
MONTAGE: Administration Building. Agricultural Building. Court
of Honor. Grand Basin.
INSERT: *"Street in Cairo."*
EXTERIOR: Egyptian Pavilion
HUSBAND: *(With brochure)* Oriental dancing its called. Come on.
WIFE: No. Its that uncorseted shimmy-shake.
HUSBAND: No. They do it in the Middle East.
WIFE: & I think they use snakes.
HUSBAND: No. Its like a folk dance.

WIFE: Belly dancing.
HUSBAND: All the — *"Exotic"* folks do it.
WIFE: *Kutchy kutchy.*
HUSBAND: Egyptians and them.
WIFE: Not us.
HUSBAND: But . . .
WIFE: Come along!

INTERIOR: Egyptian Pavilion
Admission $1.10

Slow Pan: the delight of *shock & scandalized* faces under derbies,
bowlers, fedoras, top hats & caps; elbow to elbow, hip to hip.
ESTABLISHING SHOT: *"The foreign exotic dancing girls."*
WELLBOURNE: For the second time that day I. M. Wellbourne, gentle-
man, stands, astounded, immobile as a pillar of salt.
Does not, or, cannot, or, wills to not to believe
what he, but one among the crush, gawks at,
as she,

"Little Egypt," née "Mahszar,"
or "Fahrida Spyropolos,"
or "Fatima," or whoever "she" is,
or we think her to be;
if she is an actual is;
& is not a figment;
        teases,
hips rippling, like Muybridge's flipping photographs,
        near popping at each stop like the shine's shine rag;
slithers,
with an ease of *"bodily contractions"*;
as if aided by the newly invented zipper

("Automatic, Continuous Clothing Closure,"
patent 1851),
twists;

in a manner *"unrefined"*;
out of her beaded halter & skirt.
These hips' weaving-waving *Danse du Ventre*;
with "hideous yodeling," ringing finger cymbals;
startlingly staccato made-up-at-the-moment
writhing tambourine's rhythms,
—like the boot black's shine-rag
hypnotic as her layered veils swirls;
is not empirical, not rational, not proper dance.
Dance is the art of precise, expressive,
graceful human movement,
as done by pearl skinned American girls.

A Wellbourne fear:
the dark spirit & matter of these new so-called amusements are the
camel's nose under the tent flap;
hopes it can be contained;
fears foreign elements & techniques will wheel about, turn about,
foster emotions wild & uncontrollable;
hopes they will be noted by little more than scattered smatterings of
the masses massed at the fair;
fears the improvisational ability to simultaneously communicate
the form's passion & pulse will evolve over time into an infectious
outbreak, raise the national temperature to a fever pitch & the camel,
humps & all, will be in the tent.
Fears it will be a *"a national calamity,"* awakening even darker forces,
& wield considerable influence of their own, marking in their own
ragged way, the under-rumbling of Change. Innovation. Conversion.
Reformation. Foster transition to the rapid spread

of the public epidemic of dark exotic eroticism to a rhythm foreign to
our *Hup* 2 *three* four.
Then there will be no keeping them.

Flash forward:
2 years hence, Wellbourne, at a dinner party pitched
by P. T. Barnum's grandson & heir. Witness "Fahrida Mahszar,"
or "Fatima," or whoever "she" is.
Cavorting her solo improvisational Rags Sharqi on a table top.
She is sans scarf, halter, veils, belt, skirt, sequins,
or beads. She is nude; not a fiber, not a stitch, not a rag.

The Columbian World's Exposition's slogan claimed,
"The Whole World Will Be There"

But not, Wells, Ida B. (1862–
1931), civil rights advocate harked,
Afro-Americans, the creators of A-
MERICA's wealth but not its possessors, or the
bearers of the dignity that accompanies it.
Nor, she said, would they even be welcomed celebrants,
as they had not been its planners, workers or
exhibitors; would be, at best, strangers within
the White City's gates. Said, she wasn't buying
into it & no others of the race should
swallow it either. Be nothing, Wells, the child
of slaves, orphaned at 14, aided in the raising
of 5 younger siblings, crusading journalist
& uncompromising combatant against lynching,
protested, nothing but A-merica's coming out
party, a gussied up presentation of the
same old stereotype stew; "uncivilized
coloreds" served in a new shiny white basin.

Be involved, Douglass countered.

Brother Douglass
& sister Wells represented 2 sides of the
question of colored involvement in the unfair
affairs of the Fair.
                    He, as Hayti's
representative, with his bust in the
Pavillon Haitien, & chairman of the Fair's
Afro-American Jubilee Day Committee,
a set-aside day "for the use and pleasure
of the colored people of the United States."
Involvement meant a chance to show their dignified side.
To be living demonstration of the quarter
century of progress since emancipation.

Despite generation & gender differences,
united in their anti lynching crusading
they showed their oppressors a single face.
Together Wells & Douglass produced the
Fair condemning pamphlet,
The Reason Why the Colored American
"Is Not in the World's Columbian Exposition."
(The tract financed not by the black middle class,
in their fear, but by church women in their faith.)

A shortlist of the present-day black better known
others (sisters & brothers) truckin' through the turnstiles:
James Weldon Johnson, Henry Ossawa Tanner,
Paul Laurence Dunbar, Booker T. Washington &
George Washington Carver.

Come "Colored People's Day," Friday, August 25th 1893:
500 voice children's choir followed addresses
& prayer at Douglass's Colored People's Day. Then
European classical chorals by 100
fifty adult musicians & vocalists. Then
The Fisk Jubilees sang Negro spirituals. Then
recitations by Miss Hallie Q. Brown, noted

elocutionist & distinguished race woman,
& Paul Laurence Dunbar, poet. Dunbar (18-
72–1906), sounding, in his
"Columbian Ode" composed for the Fair, like the
"soft tongued apologist" he praised Douglass for not
being, wrote of the growth of A-MERICA from
a *"tangled waste"* to a place that *"Now teems with men
of Nature's noblest types."* He hailed Columbus *"That
mighty mariner, the Genoese,
who dared to try."*
Douglass rose. Spoke. *"We Negroes love our country.
We fought for it. We ask only that we be treated
as well as those who fought against it."*
Questioned whether A-MERICA had *"honesty enough,
loyalty enough, honor enough,
patriotism enough to live up to their
own Constitution. . . . We intend that the A-
merican people shall learn of the brotherhood
of man and the fellowship of God from our presence
among them."*

       Wells, applauded, gave Douglass
a heart felt thank you for his leadership.

Note: That day the Fair's management, without consulting
Douglass, proving it lacked honesty, loyalty or humanity enough,
placed watermelons around the grounds of the White City for
coloreds, in the pleasure of their leisure, to *"appropriate."*

Douglass & Wells' partnership can be counted
as an early fulfillment of Cleveland's keynote
invocation. They held fast to the goal
which underlay their struggle. They let their hopes &
aspirations *"wake forces which in all time to come
influenced the welfare, the dignity & the
freedom of mankind."*

Change
was upon A-merica, yet most were unaware.
Most still hear the up beat down beat, as over
the course of the Exposition the rich get richer,
the poor need more, *ONE*, 2, *THREE*, & Time & The Press
& Church & State & the millions of A-merican
consumers, the A-MERICANists, forward march,
UMPH! umph! UMPH! & ratatatta,
but Change is up-
on A-merica despite the best wishes &
minds of the Good White Race of their generation.
Note: Remember Comte de Buffon from way back talking 'bout
time & change & like that: *"Never think that God's delays are God's
denials. Hold on; hold fast; hold out. Patience is genius."* Remember it.
Note: In contemporary fantasy a blown away little white girl
from middle A-merica leads a trio looking for what's lacking in their
lives. They trek through a color caste system up a golden road to
nowhere.
Of her backup, 1 lacks a brain, a 2nd a heart & the 3rd courage.
They're recruited by the total humbug leader to fight his fight.
Getting their wishes granted is to be their reward. Their assignment,
should they decide to accept it, is to bump off a rival haling from way
out west, clothed in black & branded as wicked. Gullible as gobblers
they buy it. Doo Dah. & indeed do the deed.
All's well that ends with a click of the heels of her shiny shoes & she's
right back where she started but wiser &
better for it. Ah, but it was just a dream,
a dream she had on her mind.
The tale concocted by Frank Baum (1856–1919), journalist, actor,
axle grease salesman, opera house owner, author son of a women's
rights activist & an oil magnate & theater chain proprietor. Baum
a man of many literary faces: Floyd Akers, Schuyler Staunton, &
Edith Van Dyne, wrote the Wizard of Oz tales to teach sincerity,
independence, honesty & bravery: good old solid as a rock so-
called A-merican values. Baum attended the World's Columbian
Exposition. Was the color caste White City featuring defective
Others was the inspiration for the Emerald City of Oz.

Change was upon America.

& though smothering under the legacy of lack & an endowment of
inequity, the form & force of ragtime, still nearly nameless, flickers
in the tinderboxes of the dis-reputable good time establishments
of commerce & joy in the coal black sections of off-Mississippi
rail towns like St. Louis & Sedalia: the music sanctums & pools
halls, saloons & poontang parlors. Smoldering, fueled by the fever
of defiance & the intensity of need, it nears full heliotropic plume
& wafts from under doors & through chinks & cracks & up the
chimneys, signaling a change in the atmosphere that will release a
heat & light-like combustion so intense its miasmic fallout will be
like an exhalation from the fiery belly of the beast of the Industrial
Revolution.

CHAPTER
14

 The Buffalo Bill Show's

Rough Ride Across the Bridge

from Old History to New Myths,

Featuring Annie Oakley, Sitting Bull,

Queen Victoria & Walt Whitman

Cross cut: outside the Fair grounds.

 Cross cut: Outside the grounds of the sprawling Buffalo Bill Show, close enough to The White City to benefit by proximity & compete for the discretionary leisure dollar.

WELLBOURNE:
Woozy, his feet hot, tired, watches the unsupervised
dark eyed foreigners, sweat-wage hirelings & less-fettered
coloreds swagger, raucous, through the post bellum streets
of abject infamy, humming, whistling, fiddling,
dancing, singing, fabricating gerrymandered
enclaves of self-determined fun.
Change was upon A-merica,
& it was not without form, for upon its face & its Spirit
It was hot & it was dark.

Wellbourne enters

BUFFALO BILL'S
WILD WEST CONGRESS
OF ROUGH RIDERS
Of The
WORLD

AMERICA'S FAMILY SHOW

Since 1823

"America's National Entertainment"

but judged too lowbrow to share in the Fair,
opens with his Cow-Boy Band's rendition of
the Star Spangled Banner.

Note: Its melody appropriated by Francis Scott Key's (1779–
1843) from the English drinking song.

Buffalo Bill
William Frederick Cody, a.k.a. *"Buffalo Bill"* [1846–1917], the Wild
West's showmanship answer to P. T. Barnum. Former frontier army
scout & buffalo killer for the railroads & theatrical performer.
That
combination
again —
show business &
"history" maker.
Liberty taker. Fact faker. Truth shaker. Reality breaker.
Cody.
Known.
Far. Wide.
Revered.

Top. Bottom.

Side to side.

Endeavored, while playing (nudge nudge) cowboys & Native
Americans, in his How the West Was Won fable, to manufacture,
for the consumptive pleasure of eagerly paying Eastern pale faces, a
sanitized, homogenized, romanticized redskin product as needsome
& to their liking, as had been the line of meek & contented coons
contrived for them during Minstrelsy. A double-faced sleight of
hand that abracadabraed the cowboy from its farthest back notion
of a Revolutionary War bunch, *"who were exceedingly barbarous in the
treatment of their opponents,"* into the symbol of the A-merican pioneer
spirit & can-do character; even wholesome, with just the hint of an
edge: *"A man employed to take care of grazing cattle on a ranch ... and
leads a hard rough life, which tends to make him rough and wild in character"*
(O.E.D.). With Bill himself the most symbolic of the symbols &
shining star of stars.

Carefully self-concocted mixture of smooth & rough, charm &
mayhem, savvy & myth, show & man, then & now; any how they
wanted,

whatever they needed at whatever time.

+ cast of an amalgam of 600:

Scouts & Soldiers, Cossacks & Gauchos & Russians, Arabs,
Filipinos, Puerto Ricans, Arapahos & Cheyenne & Sioux ... &
400 horses starring in his "historical" show of life on the range,
homestead; buffalo hunt; pony express, stage coach robbery; loads of
horse riding, roping & racing, rooting, tooting & shooting & parades
with military pomp, plus a prime attraction,

Annie Oakley, née Phoebe Mozee, a.k.a. Mauzy, a.k.a. Mosey, a.k.a.
Moses (1860–1926).

"The Peerless Lady Wing-Shot."

With hourglass figure, but prim & refined as a parson's wife;
packaged her as the woman of the Western Plains,
but 'd been born & reared in the Ohio woods,
Doodah,
& had, like Bill before her,
killed to earn her daily bread.

Strung on her belt, wild fowl'd swung,
feathered testaments to steely hand & eye sure as shooting.
She could & did with shotgun or sidearm
perforate a playing card's heart,
plug falling dimes—from 30 yards away,
shoot the ash off a cigarette,
shatter tossed clay pigeons to dust
& colored glass balls the size of tangerines
to a sparkling shower,
like confetti from a rainbow.
                    "Little Sure Shot"
Sitting Bull said of her. Annie (nudge nudge) hit the spot.

Picture
one of Bill's *"dramatic spectacles"*:
the prairie:
little house. *"Settlers."*
Young Ma, with hair the color of noon straw,
the young'n's,
Pa, solid as his clenched jaw
peaceful as Sunday pie.
Of a sudden a cyclone of dust:
full tilt stampede of unprovoked
blood-curdling yelping, circling,
near naked, bronze, painted faced demon bucks attacking
thick & fast in full hostility.
Boo. Hiss. Sweeps the crowd like small pox.

Savage red savages savaging innocent, put upon white homesteaders
seeking simply to settle, the announcer megaphones.

Smoke. Flames. Mayhem.
Hiss. Boo.
Then: *"Buffalo Bill"*
(played by Colonel W. F. Cody himself),
"The dime novel brought to life,"
enters.

In skin tight breeches of velvet,
his buckskin top tailored, fringed & embroidery beaded;
mustached, goateed.
Widebrimmed, dashingly angled Stetson.
"Putting on style," as he called it.
For them to reckon was that *"putting on"*
like in fronting, adding airs, frills?
Or, like a pretended, a feigned outward appearance.
A put on act to mislead or amuse?
A buckra in buckskin?
Works both ways he thinks as he
circles the arena at an urgent canter now,
once around, hat aloft, silken curls shoulder length
luft like lace curtains.
Posture perfect.
Enchanted intake in the collective chest, breast & throat
like children at Christmas.

Wellbourne pictures
Messiah
mounted
on a hand-tooled saddle;
God at a gallop
one time around.
A stir in the gentlemen & ladies alike.
Then, stillness. Within it
at the dead silence of the 1, 2, 3, 4 of the tom toms
they had not thought to hear above their heartbeats.
Bill at full dash dissects the circle
with a whoop,
swoops in the flash of an eye
flings himself from his saddle
quick & sure as a streak of righteous lightning.

The crowd, its collective breath released, gasps.
Bill, "like a spirit" darts
"with Grace and Skill"

into the heart of the dangerous undertaking
to, with Bowie bared, six-shooter blazing & fists,
commence battling red devils swarming like wild-fire,
left, right & 2 ways from Sunday,
dispensing hand-to-hand white man to red man justice.
Unprompted the crowd whoops & screams
like banshees at a bier.
Badly outnumbered too many to 1
it bodes black for Bill,
but for the last minute charge
in splendid style of the posse of the cowboy gallants
onto the grounds,
accompanied by the brass back-up
of Bill's 27 man band
& the customers' (including Wellbourne's)
shared relieved sigh.
The renegades, to their grief,
recognize to their dismay
they've run against Buffalo Bill & his rough riding,
hard working, deft & fearless cow-boy cavalry.
There ensues between the punchers, hands & drovers
& the blood-thirstys
a cloud of confusion & cut throat chaos.
Let them hear your encouragement, ladies & gents!
They ratchet their cheers up a notch or 2.
In ritualistic mano a mano revenge following the Little Big Horn, as
he told it, Buffalo Bill killed & scalped native American leader Yellow
Hand. "The 1st scalp for Custer!" Bill boasted.
A roar. Whoops! Louder:
Bill & his boys triumph,
3 cheers.
rescuing the poor colonist's scalp
Hip Hip
& saving the day by repulsing,
in the name of the A-merican way,
the uncivilized squaw men
Hooray! Hip Hip

to their Happy Hunting Grounds.

God Bless America!

& in the reconstructed telling turned Custer's attempted genocidal land grab & subsequent suicide by self aggrandizement, into a patriotic pop fare stage play for the consumption of the paying public.

It stirred Mark Twain *"like a war song."*

That's Entertainment!

All in all, the announcer declares,

preventing the massacre by the blood-thirstys.

Let's hear it for Buffalo Bill!

They went wild.

Hurrah. & alleluia.

& alleluia again.

Justice administered to the invaders

(nudge nudge) in a language they understand.

A-merica is safe, Wellbourne thinks,

for A-merican democracy. Hurrah.

& alleluia.

Yes, Wellbourne thinks, buoyed, beaming.

Bill saved the day!

"Gunpowder entertainment" at its very best,

In so many words the hen-pecked husband

Pulled reluctantly from the Egyptian Pavilion

on the street in Cairo

nudges his wet-eyed wife.

Y'know, he found out what we wanted, how we wanted it &

gave it to us just that way, hey hey.

Us: good.

Them: bad.

Us: noble.

Them: savage.

Us: peaceful.

Them: warlike.

Us: Us.

Them: Them, drunks, dog eaters, tribal, sneaky, primitive, beaked

noses, eagle eyes, dirty, lazy, wife beaters, ignorant, degenerates,
raiders, ambushers, uncouth, cowards, a curse, Injuns.
Us: Yes.
Them: No.
Till it's as plain as —
as — red & white.
Or,
as Mencken, H(enry) L(ouis), 1880–1956, American humorist out
of Baltimore, famously said, *"No one ever went broke underestimating the
intelligence of the American public."* Cody didn't. Though, his P.R., as
Barnum's before him, spun it as to help it go down smooth & easy
as winking (nudge nudge).
wholesome, educational.

Alleluia & Yee Haw.
Featured in the show was chief Sitting Bull,
a.k.a. Tatanka-Iyotanka (1831–1890)
signed on, with a $125.00 bonus, for $50 a week,
& a performing pony at contract's end; Tatanka-Iyotanka with Crazy
Horse (1842–1877) and Ogalaga, guided their people to victory
against General George Armstrong Custer's cavalry at the Battle of
the Black Hills Little Bighorn in '76. Upon making the acquaintance
of the White Mother, a.k.a. Queen Victoria, told him, *"I would not let
them take you around in a show like this."*
But he belonged to him self did Tatanka-Iyotanka.
Was a Hunkpapa Sioux. A holy man. Hold onto our land, he advised
his people. The encroaching, buffalo slaughtering, gold lusting,
genocidal American-ists are coming, but, Wovoka (a.k.a. Jack
Wilson) (c. 1856–1932), a Paiute mystic, had fashioned a new ritual.
We've got to Ghost Dance our troubles away, he said. They tried.
Tried, thinking after the 5th day of hypnotic-trance-dancing the

whites would disappear. Happy days would be theirs again, spirits would be renewed, ancestors resurrected, they would live forever with more than enough for all.

The Ghost Dance didn't do the trick.

Being out manned, outgunned & hemmed in they gave up the ghost; climbed, with resigned embarrassment, as show Indians aboard Cody's bad history bandwagon. & did, for wages & to see the world, blushful reenactments of their former fiery selves.

In the doing not only lost their chance to write history, but, in that fool's-gold standard that of gilt by association way that passes for proof amongst hucksters & the free to be fleeced, they authenticated Bill's novel hokey-fiddling of the West's legend & legacy, prime proof to the out-easterners there was peace on the fearsome prairie outskirts of civilization, the renegade redskin coyotes were defanged; were sheep; sheared, in the good guys' time & on their terms, by the might of A-merica's Destiny Manifested.

The romance of the frontier found its form; was in its season. *"Let my show go on!"* were Colonel Bill's dying words.

Sitting Bull was as stubborn as his name implies, yas yas & bad to the bitter end. "I am not going. Do with me what you like. I am not going. Come on! Come on! Take action! Let's go!" he said being killed by federal troopers while "resisting arrest."

Crazy Horse's last words, unrecorded, came as he was knifed to death while trying to escape a federal prison. "We've got them!" Custer, with Columbus like foresight, bragged, as he gave up the ghost.

The USS Crazy Horse, a starship in the Star Trek fleet, honors his name.

Columbus has cities, rivers & parks named in his honor, Doodah.

CHAPTER
15

 The Long March of Change Continues

Vaudeville Arrives, Booker T. Washington,

W. E. B. Du Bois & the Blues (at Their

Beginning) Return & Rag's Infection

Rages, as We Consider Voodoo,

Thermodynamics & Continue to Hear

Dead People & Living Spirits

1898–1900

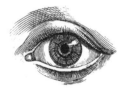

EYE OF THE BLACK VOICE:
Look on **1898:**
See a change on the Great White Way.
See blacks light out for that storied territory.
See the 1st black written & produced Broadway
musical: *"A Trip to Coontown"* truckin' with a load
of taxing whitemen's baggage rattling along
behind. To be disgorged, they hoped, along the rocky,
uncharted road to Show Business wonder as

opportunity enabled. See the likes of
Robert "Bob" Cole (1868–
1911), Billy Johnson (c.
1858–1916), & Paul
Laurence Dunbar open the gates to a long march
of unbound colored talent.

PADDY:
'Tis as if rag-time is a force & influence
unwittingly & unwillingly called forth by
President Cleveland "which in all time to come shall
influence mankind." Maybe for his own & our,
his constituents', the Americanists
consumers, sake he would've been better served if
he'd left the lid on that black box, left the veil un-
lifted, let sleeping forces lie. Calling for
creation is like calling down the fire.
Either, upon igniting, spreads beyond the will
or skill of its evokers or practitioners
to contain its defiant consumption. &
what's to be done with these all black black minstrels who
trespass against the Good Old Way It Was? Has good
old blackened faced MINSTRELSY been ragged into the pale?
Have these black black minstrels ruined MINSTRELSY for all?

RASTUS:
(Smirking)
Seems these blackened faced white aspiring
A-mericanists are too busy failing at
being colored to matter any more. Ha ha.

PADDY:
(Whisper)
Is
(Gasp)
Blackened faced white minstrelsy
(Shudder)

Dead?

VOICE OF THE BLACK EYE:
Change is upon A-merica.
Change.
Energy. Conversion. Transformation. At all
points of contact; flashpoints on multi-fronts.
    Change is upon A-merica.

See Walt Whitman, U.S. poet, carpenter, celebrant of universal
brotherhood, sexuality & democracy, wearer of his slouch hat as he
pleased, indoors or out. Seated, listing slightly left, vested, rumpled
jacketed, white shirt opened at the collar. His beard like ocean waves
crashing against a rocky crags of his cheeks.

WALT WHITMAN:
(Incanting from his poem "Reversals")
"Let that which stood in front go behind,
Let that which was behind advance to the front,
Let bigots, fools, unclean persons, offer new propositions,
Let the old propositions be postponed."

VOICE OF THE BLACK EYE:
Change is upon A-merica.

Critiquing Whitman, Greek born, wholly malcontented, partially
blind, husband of a Japanese wife from a samurai family, U.S.
journalist & author Lafcadio Hearn (1850–1904) says, *"Mr. Whitman's*
muse is at once indecent and ugly, lascivious and gawky, lubricious and coarse."
Oscar Wilde, née Fingal O'Flahertie Wills (1854–1900), Anglo-Irish
playwright. Author. Poster boy for *"The Love that dare not speak its*
name" & wit, wrote in contradiction, saying of Whitman, *"He has begun*

a prelude to larger themes. He is the herald to a new era."
Change is upon A-merica at all points of contact.
Like evolution, like from 1 stage to another, like postulated by
French naturalist, Jean-Baptiste Pierre Antoine de Monet, Chevalier
de Lamarck (1744–1829) & picked up on & developed by British
naturalist Russel Wallace (1823–1913) & Charles Darwin—like
how survival was about adapting to the setting, like the process of
the slow & steady when some thing changes into some thing more
multifaceted & better. *"Historians will have to face the fact,"* Austrian
ethnologist Konrad Lorenz (1903–1989) said, *"that natural selection
determined the evolution of cultures in the same manner as it did that of species."*
      Yas yas,
the change of cultures & things cultural, like blacks about-facing the
notion of acquired characteristics that blackened faced Daddy Rice
& his knot of shams had pimped since the 1830s &, in the doing,
rousting that mishmash of faux niggers from the entertainment
woodpile & sending them pratfalling on their deceitful white rumps.
& *"If your buttocks burn,"* to quote an apartheidistic white South
African proverb, *"you know you have done wrong."* Doodah. Oh, yeah?
Like blacks who had been repeatedly dirty done? & continued
grabbling between exclusion & inclusion, this time as minstrelsy
gadded to the next stage.
(Nudge nudge)
Vaudeville,
birthed in barrooms, takes its toddling baby steps.
In its natal form the slap-dashed, half faced
bastard child mirrors its blackened faced minstrel sire.
Fruit don't fall far from the tree, see. But its desire:
be not base; rise higher; aspire, claim, with
Barnumesque straight face, its legitimacy. Not
just fare for the foul, the low, the common, but
be banquet for the new egalitarian
families' varied appetites; democratic
diversion-consumables to sate cravings of
every A-merican & ethnic of every
cast & ambition, with the price of admission.
Caricature continued as the standard

of the day—but, & a very big but it is,

in a more . . . respectable way, say.
The afore mentioned but, as noted, was a Hottentot Venus sized butt.
See Saarjite Baartman, South African Khoisan woman caged, naked,
exhibited, as a visual aid for the sexual freaks savage color women
were, throughout narrow ass Jolly Ol' foggy 19th century England
& froggy (as Brits deemed anyone distasteful to them) France, *"OH!
Rien de Dieu quel boeuf de rôtis! N'est pas?"* "OH! My God what a lot of roast
beef! Is it not?" François indique, being frank.

Vaudeville could, safely, feature white women now, now that
renderings of blackened faced males were no longer the main
attraction sucking in the bucks.
Fret not, more modern methods of racist
characterization await their cue,
eager for their entrance & center stage.

Meanwhile,
down in deep Dixie, in cotton fields, at barn &
tin-topped shack-backs, in thin & thicket & pit
of night, capital B Blues, before it has its name,
peck & scratch 'bout to hatch into the beck & call
of hope & thrall: see the moon-silhouetted man
bowed over his self-made guitar; hear him with the
rhythm of his groan, grunt & sigh set loose a
quavering wave of bent, slurred & spaced air through
the box of cartilage & membrane, & hear the
answering Amen as knotted bones & skin pluck
& strum cords of wire affixed to a box of wood.
Hear (re)new(ed) pulses clinching & surging on the

continuing flow of the notion of long dis-
covery; (en)lightening Dark Forces. In chanted
harmony an owl barks, a hound hoots; the night
shivers, its tones & overtones resonating.
It will move, like a runagate; steady foot pats
a pulsation that resound its liberating
Ju Ju in ripples of delight & comfort
to those below & above the parallel at
39° 43' N,
Yas yas.
The new white-nigger working class chimney-sweeps,
shinny men, hod-toters, muck shovelers, peddlers,
laundresses amongst them, know not of the forming
forms' kinship to Rag, nor what it can do for them
'gainst the damp & gnarled of their wearisome being.
But, Doodah da, A change was upon even them.

Though, alas & alack, for every Afro A-
merican step forward there was a shuffle slide
back: Look back on **1895** & hear ol'
Jim Crow's postulates of separation sanctioned by
Booker T.'s Cotton State & International
Exposition, a.k.a. Atlanta Expo,
allocution. See Booker Taliaferro
Washington (1856–1915),
American slavery-born educator.
See him in tattersall vest & tailcoat of the
sort favored by the Kingfish. Imagine him going
into his stretch, do a high, leg-kick windup, hurl
one through the heart of the zone right by Andy
H. Brown, who in his gullibility does not
even get his bat off his shoulder, does not, in
fact, even see the pitch. Watch Washington praise
the South for allowing coloreds the chance to
"dignify and glorify common labour."
"Nothing," says he in conclusion, *"in thirty years*
has given us more hope and encouragement, and

drawn us so near to you of the white race, as this opportunity offered by
the Exposition."

Note: Washington was the only African American invited to
speak. Doo dah.

"We
can be
as separate as the fingers,
yet
one as the hand," he says. His pitch to the Expo's
assembled was *"received with favour and*
enthusiasm" by the audience . . . largely
composed of the most influential class of white
men and women. See in their grand majesty, the
nine jimcrowphobes cloaked in black robes agree
& hand down the deep dyed & certified decree:
Plessy v. Ferguson,
"separate

but equal"

(Hah Hah).

See post-war coonosity legalized
all over God's land, & once alchemized from base
concept to golden concrete, see negroes as the
legitimately, officially, disenfranchised.
Doodah. Judicially & in the court of
public opinion, almost right back where they started.
Laughingstock. *"Once victim, always victim —*
that's the law!" wrote Susan Sontag, essayist
(1933–2004).

RASTUS:
I am, as Shakespeare said, *"a man more sinned*
against than sinning." Witness A-mericanists still,

even though, or perhaps because, the mask has been
cast aside, perpetuate Minstrelsy's magic
notion of crude negritude; that, Yes, coons is, how-
ever tragic,

still
aimless,
shameless,
blameless buffoons.

VOICE OF THE BLACK EYE:
But God's delays are not God's denials
& change is on America:
In the late '90s
John Philip Sousa & Victor Herbert
widen their net, commandeer Cuban
rhythms, go shamelessly public with *"El Capitan"*
& *"Cuba Song"*

on & on. & on to **1899.**
See
Du Bois look on a lynched colored man's body parts
displayed trophy-like in an Atlanta barber
shop's window. See Du Bois weep. Unashamedly,
like self-blinded Oedipus howling at the cross-
roads, moons & miles from Colonus. See Du Bois forge
his no head ducked tail tucked position on the Race
Problem. Witness, as he does, A-merica's con-
tinued intoxication with the new leisure-
era amusement of Ragtime.

See,
in tipped bowler & box-backed jacket, the so-called
ragtime professor, stogie a slow-drag metronome
to the waddle & twist of the working girl's wig-
wagging up to her crib; the john, in keen
anticipation, glides wobble-kneed up behind.

In passages that rival his tune's rhythmic
raunch the professor's lissome fingers also
tickle lithe changes as light on the ivories
as the silk chemise slides on the young chippie's
powdered haunch.
                    Yas yas.

RAGTIME PROFESSOR:
Ragtime is an abundance in an abundant
time. A cornucopia of vaudeville tunes &
Minstrel songs waggle-staggering over dis-
located accents ragged & colored in content
as a coon's behind.

VOICE OF THE BLACK EYE:
—But, can you say SYN'CO-PAT'ED? Up-beat. Yas yas.

RAGTIME PROFESSOR:
They think: Rag is just white music in Black Face! No
no!

VOICE OF THE BLACK EYE:
Ragtime catches the common ear, catches like
lightning in a crock, catches the make-up & high
spirits of the new All A-mericanist. Yas
yas.

RAGTIME PROFESSOR:
Thanks to steps forward in speed of production &
haulage there are things in their amplitude: an out-
pouring, a spate; scads, heaps, oodles, bumper crop,
profusion, feast.
                    Consumerism & our rag-
time portend & enormous time shift & shift(s) in
time(s), celebrating the new U S of A, while
(nudge nudge & a wink of the eye) mocking the very
notion of the strict 4/4 of all all A-

merican music & its tradition &
patriotic intent to move (nudge nudge) the masses—
Oomph Oomph Oomph Oomph—in an ordered & orderly
lock-step.
        Rag-time is a sniggle that'll release a
suppressed giggle'll wiggle, like an eel, in the
throes of a wriggle, down the body till their toes
jiggle in a manner "unrefined." Yas yas. It
is that "weird and intoxicating effect" in
plain sight, but, they think, hidden behind our scrim of
exotic, naughty, negro bawdy & played, they
pretend, for laughs, nudge nudge & a wink of the eye . . .
Our ragtime becomes, in effect & in fact, their
music; The Craze. Uprights are purchased, piano
rolls & banjos snapped up like Sambo's tiger-buttered
hot cakes. They dance. Fox & turkey trot & cakewalk
'round ball-rooms & social clubs.

VOICE OF THE BLACK EYE:
Change is upon A-
merica.

RAGTIME PROFESSOR:
"If I could blow a horn and lead a circus band,
Say wouldn't it be a dream,
If coons could only rule this great United Land,
Say wouldn't it be a dream . . ."
Bob Cole's ragtime lyrics joked, or did they?
                             Howsomeever,
was all in a day's labor as practiced by us
colored, time-altering piano professors
playing our seductive & seditious work, yas
yas.
        Spirit artisans we. Quintessence smelters.
Root forgers. Substance smiths. (If its a western or classical equivalent
you seek think Hephaestus,
he-FESS-tus) *Greek* god, lame, with halting step—uh oh—more

wheel about & turn about! —or Vulcan,
his Roman variant. Overseers of *tech-
nology, craftsmen,* working with *fire* & things
too hot for others to handle. Yas yas yas.

I speak here, of course, of work in the Hoo-Doo sense.
Laying of tricks: stealth of candle burning, goofer
dust, crossroads convenings, spells cast & countered sort
of messing with the mind, work. Yas yas.

VOICE OF THE BLACK EYE:
     Will be
Carl Jung'll make up analytical psychology,
collective unconscious, shadow self & about
how race & culture cloud 1 & all's minds.
       Jung'll
say, *"Masses are always breeding grounds of psychic
Epidemics."*
      But, well, hell, we knew that; back from
way back. Back from buckras to Barnum drumming &
fifing & trumping up holier & haughtier
than "them" notions into the noggins of nations
of sleepwalkers & locksteppers, in seduced states
of 1 track narcotization, flocking along
at their bogus bandmasters' beck, in, sheep-like
4/4 formation step for step.
        But look on what
our Ragged-time can cause when we snatch
back the scrim from Minstrelsy's blackened faced black
vizard of awes
      —an epidemic—
exposing
the dark humbug of the masked desires of all A-
mericanist consumers. Their only cure is
to be disabused of their notion of in-
fallibility & superiority—

& cross the bridge to reconnection with common
humanity.

RAGTIME PROFESSOR:
'S why we're ragging it (& by our attitude &
act bragging it) & sure 'nough unknotting
the nation sack; letting the black cat out the bag,
so to speak. Rousing them into a new trance dance
& bringing 'bout, Oou, hot damn! carousing change. Rag-
time's catchy, catching offbeat 2 faced, double edged
contagion & tonic is infectious as fear
or fun. Swift, broad & effective, its morbific
spread, Yas Yas, simultaneously affects Hosts
of hosts. We black practitioners, do a switcheroo —
feed a fever to starve a cold. & we, with all the
Time in the world in our hands & on our side, take
our own sweet, tricky, transposing time laying down
a squabble of discord wit' dese crafty
chords, Yas yas, to upset their peaceful mind, while
making 'em twist & grind in syn-co-pated time.

PADDY:
(Unaware, as always, of the irony)
What's best to rid us of this vermin? How can the
epidemic be stopped?

I. M. WELLBOURNE ET AL.:
(As they then hightail it out of there)
It has to do with the contagion
in the air.
The scourge of ragging is widely prevalent
among the lower & low-mid working classes,
their constitutions having been weakened by their
former addiction to the hypnosis like state
of obtuseness, or waking sleep, which rimes with sheep,
of minstrelsy. So infectious it is it has
no regard for race.

VOICE OF THE BLACK EYE:
Rag—

IT
IS HOT! in
effect
& in
fact. Hot & dark.

PRAGMATISTS & SCHOLARS & POLITICIANS & THEM:
(From behind their screen of the so-called "scientific method")
Your claims are anecdotal. Lack (1) observation
& (2) hypothesis & (3) prediction & (4)
test & (5) retest. Don't prove a thing.
(They nod their heads & stroke their chins. Self satisfied.)

VOICE OF THE BLACK EYE:
(Eyeing them. Muses)
The *"scientific method,"* the organized set
of interrelated ideas & principles
that brought us Eugenics & Phrenology &
Drapetomania.

PRAGMATISTS & SCHOLARS & POLITICIANS & THEM:
Can you connect the dots to our satisfaction?
Provide proof for all of the above?

VOICE OF THE BLACK EYE:
I can swing it:

Dig,

Syncopation was so
so hot
it takes the recently verified 1st
& 2nd laws of thermodynamics,
discovered in 1824, the year David Walker (1785–1830),

African American, believed abolition a
"glorious and heavenly cause"; believed blood,
if necessary, should wash away the stain of slavery.
Said so in his pamphlet "Walker's Appeal"
proven in 1865
(the year of the theoretical freeing of the enslaved)
to explain how hot it is.
Syncopation, see, is energy.
Energy is the capacity to do
Work,
that is, the transference of energy
by a force acting against a body
& resulting in displacement.
Think, being able to
move
some
body, dig it?
Energy & work are measured in "foot-pounds,"
think, pounding feet, foot patting,
toe-
tapping. Heat
is a form of energy.
The kinetic energy of the said body is measured
by the temperature of that body,
i.e., of internal heat there in,
& associated with the positions
& motions
of its components;
think,
dancing. Dancing, dancing,
dancing.

The 1st thermodynamic law says
energy can be converted from 1 form
to another,
but can't be destroyed.
                              (Once

it
is
it
is. & once its motive power
is in you
it's
in you
to stay.)
&
thermodynamic law number 2 says
the spontaneity of it
turns a cold body
hot
& increases that body's dis-
order. Hence
the intoxication & jubilation of the
affected host,
which has 'em wheel about & turn about,
doing jes so. &
so
it was
that a change
was upon them.

&
it was
Hot & just as
dark.

& it
is, it
is
that the majority
of the Universe's
make-up
(nudge nudge
& a wink of the eye)

is dark.

What?

Breaks down like this:
Dark matter 25%
dark energy 70%
      but is 100% invisible, man.
Like a world of shadows & smoke(s).
This
dark matter (&
for that matter, this
matter of darkness)
that we can't see
is detectable
& evident
through the pull, e.g.,
influence
on what we can
see:
"the transference of energy
by a [dark] force acting against a body";
that is, the *"foot pounds [foot*
taps, finger snaps]"; the
kinetic
spontaneity of
wheel about &
turn about
& the Rag craze
& all dance manias to follow.
"[A] [dark] force acting against a body";
"[F]oot pounds."
"[T]ransference of energy."

It's
the very stuff of the cosmology;
Western science;

scientific explanation for all the funny stuff
been going
down.
e.g.,
the white faced fascination with Minstrelsy,
the attraction t'ward the darkness
that "inflame(s) the soul
and hypnotize(s) the minds"
& all that implied

& denied

& how come.

Think about it
the attraction to dark matter
& infections there of.

It's
even more deep-seated
than electrons, protons & neutrons.

Sun Ra, née Herman Poole Blount, a.k.a. Sonny, a.k.a.
Sun Ra, Intergalactic Arkestra leader (1915?–1993)
to whom astral voices spoke on "a space wisdom beam,"
put it this way, *"Today is the shadow of tomorrow
because coming events cast their shadow before,"* or,
what comes around has already been around.

Abe Lincoln, his top hat atip rocks. He mimes a
high 5 to Ra & says, Maybe that's why *"You can't
escape history."*

Whew!

Let's lighten up a minute (nudge nudge)
& think of it a-

nother way; take another scientific route
circulating at the end of the 19th century
& see what evolves, see if
empirically we come to the
same conclusion.

DARWIN:
(Reading from his 1859 treatise On the Origin of Species)
"Every organic being is constantly endeavoring
to increase in numbers; and . . .
if any one being
varies ever so little, either
in habits or structure . . ."

VOICE OF THE BLACK EYE:
Isn't that the substance & sum
of what we've been looking at?
The 2 faced switcheroo, white
pretending to be black?

DARWIN:
(Continuing)
". . . gains an advantage over some other inhabitant
of the same country,
it will seize on that place of that inhabitant,
however different that may be from its own place."

VOICE OF THE BLACK EYE:
Hear that?
Sound familiar?
Do' the name Daddy Rice,
or a generation or 2
of white blackened faced minstrels
ring a bell,
or conjure a parallel?
Well,
them syncopating piano professors

in their becharming badness
doctored their own signifying
wheel about on the 88s,
performing radical surgery on the coon tune sentiments,
extracting syrupy sap from High Society songs.

Operating like its payback for the years & years &
years of rotten spinning 'round getting down
picking a bale & a bale & a bale of cotton,
the ebonies & ivories jumping up & down
& snapcrackling like cat-o-9-tales
wonderworking variations on time, habit & structure,
Doodah Doodah da.
                              Say,
look forward to 1905, we're nigh there anyway, see

Elie Metchnikoff (1845–1916),
Russian zoologist riffing on immunology variations
off Darwin's survival theme.
Immunology being the biomedicine branch
concerned with the bodily distinction of self from non-self,
the
(repeating for emphasis)
self
from non-self;
real from representation.
True from portrayal,
or the combined Shadow and Act,
to borrow from Ellison, Ralph Waldo
(1914–1994), African American creator of Invisible Man,
"I am invisible, understand, simply because people refuse to see me,"
reasons his unnamed, reclaimed Br'er Rabbit-esque,

non white blackened faced Uncle Remus-ized minstrel version
of the fox flummoxing, bear bamboozling,
making his own way out of no way trickster, Honey,
nudge nudge in the wink of an eye.

METCHNIKOFF:
(Quoting himself)
"When the aggressor in his struggle
is much smaller than its adversary . . .

VOICE OF THE BLACK EYE:
Think minority.

METCHNIKOFF:
". . . the result is that the former
introduces itself into the body
of the latter & destroys it by means of infection."

VOICE OF THE BLACK EYE:
e.g.,
turns a cold body
hot
& increases that body's dis-
order. Re-
defines the elements.
Shifts accents.
Changes rhythms.

J. B. PRIESTLY:
(British author, 1894–1984)
"Out of this ragtime came the fragmentary outlines of the menace to old
Europe, the domination of America, the emergence of Africa, the end of
confidence and any feeling of security, the nervous excitement, the feeling of
modern times."

VOICE OF THE BLACK EYE:
Where's

Isadora Duncan
& what she got to say now? Oh, yeah,
the loas wrapped 'round her like boas
caught in a wheel about . . .

Something snaps!

The screen flickers whitetoblackwhitetoblackwhitetoblack
in time with the spinning real
& the broken end of the celluloid slappingslapslappingslapslapping
in syncopation . . .
As the fractured sound track:

**WILLIAM CARLOS WILLIAMS, CALVIN COOLIDGE,
IRVING BERLIN, STEPHEN DEDALUS, MANTAN
MORELAND, WILLIAM FAULKNER:**
(Shoulder to shoulder)
*"Deceive and eat." "The business of America is business." "There's no business
like show business." "History is a nightmare from which I'm trying to wake."
"How could a mess such as this happen in A-merica?" "How come it's so dark?"
"The past is never dead. It's not even past." "Deceive and eat."*

VOICE OF THE BLACK EYE:
Continues. &
Continues . . .

The A-mericanist audience shift
uncomfortably in their seats, mumble,
as if disorientated by the force,
the dynamics
of it all.
Is that smoke(s)
                    they smell?
Where did the time go?
They rise.
Don't panic,
                    they tell themselves.

Disoriented but orderly
they move toward the center. Don't
panic.
Are these the forces, they wonder,
that Cleveland meant
to be awakened by A-mericanist
hopes & aspirations?
This his intent?
This new . . . whatever it is?
This assimilation: Afro & Euro:
Rhythm & melody & harmony;
amalgamation;
combination;
permutation;
variation;
transformation;

the force
of change was upon them.

Moving up the aisle
as the curtain rings down
on the 19th century.
Orderly, but behind them
they sense something—
hot—& black—
Don't panic.
—& some substance, some-
thing they've long feared,
though did not see,
for here
in the U S of A
which, as President Cleveland also pointed out, is
"not a nation
to which peace
is a necessity."
They quicken their step,

Don't panic.
"Our hopes and aspirations
awaken[ing] forces which in all times . . .
shall . . ."

Flashback:
The blues.
　　　"The music," scholar, W. E. B.
Du Bois, says,
"of an unhappy people, of the children of
disappointment; they tell of death and suffering
and unvoiced longing toward a truer world,
of misty wanderings and hidden ways."

Flashback:
CLEVELAND:
(At the White City's opening)
"influence the welfare, the dignity,
and the freedom of mankind."

Flashback:
"God's delays are not God's denials."

VOICE OF THE BLACK EYE:
They're in a trot now.
Don't . . .
Begin to push.
　　　　　. . . panic!
What, they ask, is it that's
lurking & shaping it-
self in the backstage shadows? &
how, if it finds its form, will it,
making it up as it goes along,
act?
They hurry,
hearing the umph umph umph umph fading into
the bygone, drowned out

as the catchy new rhythm of
rags
grumble-rumble like thunder forewarning
not the gentle, metaphorical
Britannia waters-like ablution
used by Queen Anne
& her crew in Jonson's Black Masque
to cleanse themselves
of their so-called symbolic curse of blackened faced
darkness,
but a grievous, torrent of pelting hail
'bout to come pouring down on them.
They rush out into the heavy weather
of the new century,
heads covered . . .

Iris out:
Fading to
black then brown then high yellow then brown then
black again
then.
In the rush they missed the previews of coming
distractions: Montage
through the coming decade
& beyond of continuing
infectious changes wrought by
the spirit of Rag. View
of 45 starred, 13 striped Old Glory
"one Nation under God,
Indivisible, with liberty and
Justice for all" fluttering atop
the White House.
View
of Alice Roosevelt,
the Bull Moose's daughter.
"Nobody cultivates me," she claims, *"I'm wild, I'm wild."*
Princess Alice carries a stiletto in her purse. She is

caustic. Capricious & lively as the times. A wit.
"If you can't say something good about someone,"
Alice riffs, *"sit right here by me."*
She hosts a White House Valentine's dance.
Under the baton of the leader
of the United States Marine Band,
Rags are played
& Alice,
her skirt tail held high, *"kicked about*
and moves her body sinuously
like a shining leopard cat," an eye witness
witnessed & heard her sing
in a deep bass voice.
& during the next administration
buries a voodoo (the white's version
of hoodoo) doll of Helen Herron,
President Taft's wife,
in the White House lawn.

The Rough Rider himself, Teddy Roosevelt
(1858–1919),
The 26th president of the U S of A,

exhibiting, like an infection's host,
similar symptoms of a cold body turned hot &
increasing body disorder of
changes in rhythms, shifts in accents,
disruptions in time, variations in habit & structure,
"the nervous excitement,
the feeling of modern times"
hosts a White House Christmas ball.

While Juba is clapped
the leader of the Western world, Bully! Bully!
heads the shenanigans
with the charge of a high kicking
cakewalking line of dancers,
snaking like a duplicitous foreign policy
around the ball room.

Continuing
Montage of the reign of rag's cloud
of hypnotic contagion in ensuing times. View
succeeding President

William Howard Taft (1857–1930),
member of Skull and Bones, a.k.a.
The Eulogian Club,
& The Order of Death,
a Yale based secret society
whose initiation includes laying naked in a coffin,
& who Prescott Bush,
patriarch of the Bushes —
George H. W.'s father & George W.'s granddaddy —
is rumored to 've robbed, as a gift for group,
Geronimo's grave of it inhabitant's skull.
During Taft's 1st term the U.S. Marine Band
records Joplin's "Maple Leaf Rag."
When Harding names Taft
Chief Justice, the 340 lb. ex Commander in Chief,
& seventh cousin twice removed of Richard Nixon,
says, *"I don't remember
that I ever was President."*
. . . mental imperceptiveness, stupor, coma, trance . . .

View of the White House
during the upcoming Harding administration.
See what sort of leader the century wrought.
Montage:
The Navy Jazz Band playing rags &
Mamie Smith's *"Crazy Blues"*
being the 1st hit blues recording,
& speakeasies awash in Prohibition era jazz &
coonskin coats (nudge nudge) all the rage
& the 1st radio in the White House
during the *"ideal American"* Warren Harding's
"I am a man of limited talents from a small town.
I don't seem to grasp that I am president" (18-
65–1923) term (1921–1923).
Rumor had it Harding, size 14 feet, was black.
Played the cornet & was lazy,
was many babies' daddy (John Tyler held the title
with 13). Popularized *"bloviate,"*
a loud pronouncement of a pompous,
boastful statement. Remember buckra?
Lost a set of White House china
in a poker game. Said of baseball,
"There is the *soul* of the game"
(Author's emphasis).
Harding blue is a color
named for his wife who was deep
into the occult, the dark arts, you dig? Rumor
had it he paraded at least once with the Klan.
Talk about jump Jim Crow! Talk about Black Face
in whiteface & about wheel about & turn about! &
minstrelsy in the Oval Office.
"My God," he rapped,
"this is a hell of a job!"
Harding's administration
described as *"slapstick"* filled with *"buffoonery"*
(nudge nudge)
will be shadow shrouded & corruption ridden;

Big Oil kick backs
at its core.

Harry Micajah Daugherty, coiner of *"smoke filled room"*
(Smoke being a derogatory term for Negro,
Negro being a term coined to . . . well, you know . . .),
Harding's scandal scarred attorney general
tried to clear his name with a book,
"The Inside Story of the Harding Tragedy," ghosted by
— (drum roll) —
wait for it — Duh Duh —
Thomas Dixon. Author of "The Clansman"
inspiration for "Birth of a Nation."

Scene:
Hardy was in a sick bed in San Francisco.
His wife *"the Duchess,"* surnamed Kling,
who has an illegitimate child of her own
is reading dogging reviews
of his administration's first 2 1/2 years.

HARDING:
"That's good. Read some more."
(He expires.)

"Return to normalcy" was the campaign slogan
of the 29th president,
first to receive votes from women & elected with the greatest majority
vote ever achieved at the time; first to have loudspeakers at an
Inauguration, & to motor, in a Pierce-Arrow touring car, to & from
a swearing in, first to broadcast on radio; John Henry'd bills cutting
back wartime controls, immigration, taxes on the rich & showed
industry some love by raising protective tariff. Member, Phi Alpha
Delta; Knight Templar; Elk; Shriner; Freemason; Knight of Pythias

coiner of *"founding fathers,"*
is dead,

outlived by his father.

The circumstances will be baffling:
DOCTOR 1:
Blockage in the brain.

DOCTOR 2:
Extreme cardiac strain.

DOCTOR 3:
Poisoning by ptomaine.

SKEPTIC 1:	(Together)	**SKEPTIC 2:**
Suicide.		Murder.

Harding will be embalmed within 60 minutes of death.
Put on a train
for home. No autopsy was allowed.

When red headed, Vermont born on the 4th of July Vice President
Calvin Coolidge (1872–1933), who, as he would later walk his leased
pet raccoon on the White House grounds, believing *"Civilization
and profits go hand in hand,"* was asked what he thought of becoming
president said, in his voice *"about as musical as the sound made by a buzz
saw,"* *"I think I can swing it."*

Is this the end? Has dark matter spun it all out of control
for those who think themselves in control?

Is the spirit of ragtime
& all that portends
ingrained in the very marrow of A-merica?

Don't panic!

WE INTERRUPT THIS TRANS-
MISSION DUE TO TECHNICAL
DIFFICULTIES

or
is there still
color confusion
in the ranks?
A bug in the system?
A needler in the haystack?
A nigger out of the woodpile
that has jumped down & turned
the purity of FREE WHITE PERSONHOOD into a tail spin?

Say it taint so.

PLEASE STAND BY

Da-da dat
ain't
nearly all,
folks . . .

(Doodah . . .)

"In order to judge what has happened, or even what will happen, one need only examine what is happening." Buffon.

END OF REEL ONE

ILLUSTRATION CREDITS

All photographs are from the Prints and Photographs Division,
Library of Congress, unless otherwise noted.

Page 7: Karl Marx, ca. 1867. Wood engraving. LC-USZ62-16530.

Page 10: William Lloyd Garrison. Black-and-white film copy negative. LC-USZ62-10320.

Page 11: Charles Carlyle [Robert] Darwin. George Grantham Bain Collection. Digital file from original negative. LC-B2-726-1.

Page 11: Abraham Lincoln. Photograph by Alexander Gardner, 1863. Digital file from original photograph. LC-DIG-ppmsca-19301.

Page 13: Landing at Ellis Island, c. 1902. Black-and-white film copy negative. LC-USZ62-12595.

Page 21: David Livingstone. Photograph by Sophus Williams, 1884. Black-and-white film copy negative. LC-USZ62-130766.

Page 22: British Museum, London, England. Between c. 1890 and c. 1900. Views of England in the Photochrom print collection. Digital file from original. LC-DIG-ppmsc-08563.

Page 22: Jim Crow. Black-and-white film copy negative. LC-USZ62-13935.

Page 23: Crispus Attucks, "The brave soldier of the Revolutionary War, 1770," c. 1897. Copyright W. H. Curd, Chicago. Digital file from original. LC-USZ62-59669.

Page 23: Boston Tea Party massacre, March 5, 1770. Engraved, printed, and sold by Paul Revere, Boston, 1770. Black-and-white film copy negative. LC-USZ62-35522.

Page 27: William H. West's Big Minstrel Jubilee poster. Copyright 1900 by Strobridge Litho., Cincinnati and New York. Color film copy transparency. LC-USZC4-5698.

Page 38: Andrew Jackson, drawn and engraved by J. B. Longacre, c. 1815–45. Black-and-white film copy negative of cropped image. LC-USZ62-117120.

Page 41: P. T. Barnum, c. 1855–65. Brady-Handy Photograph Collection. Digital file from original negative. LC-DIG-cwpbh-02176.

Page 45: Toussaint Louverture. Black-and-white film copy negative. LC-

USZ62-7862.

Page 51: Barnum's new American Museum. Illustration in Frank Leslie's
illustrated newspaper, September 30, 1865, p. 20. Black-and-white
film copy negative of whole page. LC-USZ62-72719.

Page 55: Tom Thumb, carte de visite photograph, c. 1863. Black-and-white
film copy negative. LC-USZ62-48353.

Page 56: Man in blackface as minstrel, c. 1890–1910. Frances Benjamin
Johnston Collection. Black-and-white film copy negative. LC-
USZ62-47073.

Page 61: Plantation banjo player, c. 1875. Color film copy transparency. LC-
USZC4-2814.

Page 64: Sengbe Pieh (Joseph Cinqué), 1840. Portrait by Nathaniel Jocelyn.
Original held by the New Haven Colony Historical Society, New
Haven, Connecticut.

Page 66: Caricatures of a Negro and an Irishman evenly balanced on scale.
Illustration in *Harper's Weekly*, December 9, 1876. Wood engraving
after Thomas Nast. Black-and-white film copy negative. LC-
USZ62-57340.

Page 101: Frederick Douglass, c. 1865–80. Brady-Handy Photograph
Collection. Digital file from original negative. LC-DIG-cwpbh-
05089.

Page 104: Charles Dickens, c. 1867. Photoprint by J. Gurney & Son. Black-
and-white film copy negative. LC-USZ61-694.

Page 121: Isadora Duncan. Photograph by Arnold Genthe. From a negative
taken between 1916 and 1918. Arnold Genthe Collection. LC-
G4085-0066.

Page 124: General William T. Sherman, c. 1860–90. Engraved by John
Chester Buttre. Black-and-white film copy negative. LC-USZ62-
112190.

Page 136: Eadweard Muybridge. Frontispiece in *Animal Locomotion* by
Eadweard Muybridge (Philadelphia: University of Pennsylvania,
1887). Black-and-white film copy negative. LC-USZ62-49712.

Page 137: Animal locomotion, sixteen frames of racehorse "Annie G."
galloping, c. 1887. From Eadweard Muybridge's *Animal Locomotion*,
plate 626. Black-and-white film copy negative. LC-USZ62-52703.

Page 142: Ku Klux Klan, between 1921 and 1922. National Photo Company
Collection. Digital file from original. LC-DIG-npcc-30454.

Page 152: W. E. B. Dubois. George Grantham Bain Collection. Digital file from original negative. LC-DIG-ggbain-07435.

Page 153: Booker T. Washington, c. 1903. Copyright Cheynes Studio, Hampton, Virginia. Black-and-white film copy negative. LC-USZ62-49568.

Page 155: Warren G. Harding, 1920. Black-and-white film copy negative. LC-USZ61-177.

Page 160: World's Fair, 1893. Copyright C. C. Hyland, 1933. Panoramic photographs collection. Black-and-white film copy negative. LC-USZ62-128873.

Page 161: Grover Cleveland, c. June 1892. Copyright N. Sarony. Black-and-white film copy negative. LC-USZ62-48559.

Page 170: Little Egypt in New York, 1893. Photograph by Benjamin Falk. http://en.wikipedia.org/wiki/File:Little_egypt_dancer.JPG

Page 172: Ida B. Wells. Illustration in *The Afro-American Press and Its Editors*, by I. Garland Penn (1891). Black-and-white film copy negative. LC-USZ62-107756.

Page 178: William F. Cody ("Buffalo Bill"), c. 1911. Copyright by Moffett, Chicago. Black-and-white film copy negative. LC-USZ62-2050.

Page 184: Sitting Bull, c. 1881. Photograph and copyright O. S. Goff. Black-and-white film copy negative. LC-USZ62-12277.

Page 184: Victoria, Queen of Great Britain and Ireland, 1819–1901. Image created c. 1897. Copyright Boussod Valadon & Co. Black-and-white film copy negative. LC-USZ62-99500.

Page 188: Walt Whitman. Photograph by Gutekunst. Feinberg-Whitman Collection. Black-and-white film copy negative. LC-USZ62-92194.

Page 190: Saarjite, the Hottentot Venus (Sarah Baartman), 1811. Published by Christopher Crupper Rumford. British Cartoon Prints Collection. Black-and-white film copy negative. LC-USZ62-137332.

Page 204: Elie Metchnikoff. George Grantham Bain Collection. Digital file from original negative. LC-DIG-ggbain-14791.

Page 210: Theodore Roosevelt, c. 1902. Copyright M. P. Rice, Washington, D.C. Black-and-white film copy negative. LC-USZ62-118349.

Page 210: Alice Roosevelt, c. 1902. Photograph by Frances Benjamin Johnston. Color film copy slide. LC-USZC2-6251.

Page 211: William Howard Taft, c. 1908. Copyright G. V. Buck. Black-and-white film copy negative. LC-USZ62-48758.